UNIVERSITY COLLEGE
A Portrait, 1853-1953

UNIVERSITY COLLEGE

A Portrait

1853   *1953*

EDITED BY

CLAUDE T. BISSELL

UNIVERSITY OF TORONTO PRESS: 1953

Introductory Note

THIS VOLUME is deliberately limited in its scope. We have not attempted to write a formal history of University College. Such an undertaking would have called for a bolder search into the past, at least as far back as 1827 when Bishop Strachan obtained the charter of King's College; for a detailed analysis of the intellectual climate of the 40's and 50's when the University College idea was taking shape; and, above all, for a far more comprehensive survey of the various aspects of the College life. Fortunately, a good deal of the work has been done. *The University of Toronto and Its Colleges, 1827–1906,* and Stewart Wallace's *A History of the University of Toronto, 1827–1927* are also, in large part, histories of University College. The essay that Dr. Wallace has written for this volume is a sequel to his larger work, although it stands by itself as a guide to the main events and the principal phases of the College history. On a more modest scale than these volumes is R. A. Bell's pamphlet *The Lit: 1854–1934,* which, as a history of the oldest student society in the University of Toronto, gives many insights into the changing temper of undergraduate life, and thus supplements the fifth essay in this volume, which depends primarily on undergraduate literary journals for its record of student thought and opinion.

In thus limiting the scope of this volume, we have tried to gain something in intensity and clarity. It is our hope that the promise implicit in the title has been fulfilled and that what will emerge is, in very truth, a portrait of University College.

The contributors to this volume have been indebted to a number of people in the preparation of their essays: in particular, to Professor Eric Arthur, who generously made available some preliminary work that he had done on the University College building; to Mrs. Duncan Robertson (Barbara Browne), who did some of the research work on *The Varsity* for the essay "Opinion"; to Professor Barker Fairley and Mrs. Elsinore Haultain, who answered a number of questions about *The Rebel*.

Finally, we would express our deep gratitude to the two oldest graduates of University College—Professor Emeritus J. C. Robertson of the class of '83 and Dr. J. B. Tyrrel of the class of '80—who helped us to recreate the past of University College. In their characters and careers they symbolize that robust temper of mind and spirit that has enabled University College to contribute in generous measure to the life of Canada.

The planning and supervision of this volume have been the responsibility of an Editorial Board appointed by the University College Centennial Committee. The members of the Board were as follows: Malcolm Wallace, David Hayne, and Claude T. Bissell (Chairman)—representing the staff of University College; Mrs. V. M. Macfarlane and John W. Watson—representing the graduates; and Mrs. Duncan Robertson (Barbara Browne) and David P. Gauthier—representing the undergraduates. The Board is grateful to Mr. Hayne for undertaking to compile the Roll of Honour.

Contributors

Claude T. Bissell is Vice-President of the University of Toronto. He is also Associate Professor of English and Dean of Residence at University College.

David P. Gauthier is an undergraduate enrolled in the fourth year of Philosophy (English or History) at University College.

F. C. A. Jeanneret is Principal of University College, and Professor and Head of the Department of French.

B. K. Sandwell, formerly editor of *Saturday Night* and at present a contributor to the *Financial Post*, is one of Canada's most distinguished men of letters.

G. Stephen Vickers is Assistant Professor of Art and Archaeology in the University of Toronto.

Malcolm Wallace was Head of the Department of English in University College from 1926 to 1944, and Principal of the College from 1928 to 1944. He is now Principal Emeritus of University College.

W. Stewart Wallace is Librarian of the University of Toronto.

A. S. P. Woodhouse is Professor and Head of the Department of English at University College.

The illustrations are by Selwyn Dewdney, U.C. '31

Contents

Illustrations

xi

UNIVERSITY COLLEGE
A Portrait, 1853-1953

W. STEWART WALLACE

Background

THE HISTORY of University College is so interwoven with that of the University of Toronto that it is difficult to separate them. At times they are inseparable. But, although University College and the University of Toronto have today a common governing body (so far as finances and appointments are concerned), University College is a separate entity, with a life and history of its own—a history not without its dramatic features. Unfortunately, when, at the request of the Board of Governors of the University, I wrote my *History of the University of Toronto* over twenty-five years ago, I did not attempt to disengage the history of University College from the history of the University. The time has come to make amends for that omission.

I do not think that many graduates of University College today realize how inauspicious, how unpromising, its beginnings were. When King's College, after a brief six years of existence, came to an end in 1850, and the University of Toronto took its place, secularized and under direct government control, that dauntless old Scotsman, Bishop Strachan, promptly set to work to found the University of Trinity College. This university, the third with the founding of which Bishop Strachan had something to do (for he had been concerned with the establishing of McGill University, as well as of King's College), was opened in 1851, and the supporters of King's College promptly transferred their allegiance to Trinity. Many even of the undergraduates of King's College deserted to Trinity; and in 1852 the University of Toronto had

3

exactly one graduate in Arts—Adam Crooks, later the first Minister of Education in Ontario.

When, therefore, the University Act of 1853 brought University College into existence, as the instructional part of the University of Toronto (distinct from the University itself, which became only an examining and degree-granting body), the outlook for the newly created college was not bright. It is true that King's College had been, with its exclusively Anglican constitution, desperately unpopular; but a secular and non-sectarian college was not at that time likely to commend itself any more than King's College to large sections of the people of the Province. The fact is that most people then did not believe in the divorce of education from religion; and when Bishop Strachan described the University of Toronto as "a godless imitation of Babel" he was voicing the views of many who were not members of his own communion. The Methodists were already committed to the support of Victoria University at Cobourg, the Auld Kirk Presbyterians to the support of Queen's University at Kingston, and the Roman Catholics to the support of Regiopolis College, also at Kingston. The University Act of 1853 made provision for the affiliation of these universities and colleges with the University of Toronto, and for their representation on the Senate of the University; but not one of these institutions showed at that time any desire to take advantage of this provision. The only elements in the population of the Province who seemed likely to support University College were the Free Church Presbyterians, the Low Church Anglicans, the Baptists, the Congregationalists, and of course the atheists and the agnostics. These did not seem to promise adequate support for a college that was to be the teaching department of a provincial university.

In the matter of staff, the new college did not fare badly. The University of Toronto had taken over in 1850 practically the whole staff of King's College in Arts. The Reverend John McCaul remained Professor of Classics, and became President of the University of Toronto. He had come out to Canada in 1839 as Principal of Upper Canada College on the especial recommendation of the Archbishop of Canterbury; and this fact, as well as

certain rumours as to his royal parentage, explain perhaps his preferment in Canada, and his survival of forty years of bitter controversy over university affairs. But he was a first-class scholar, and he gained an international reputation as an authority on Greek and Roman epigraphy. The Reverend James Beaven, who had been Professor of Divinity in King's College, became Professor of Metaphysics and Ethics in the University of Toronto. Sir Daniel Wilson described him as "a dry old stick," but he was apparently not without his brighter moments, for to him is attributed one of the most famous *bons mots* in the history of the College. When some of his students installed in his chair in the lecture room the skeleton of a chimpanzee borrowed from the museum, complete with cap and gown, he remarked on entering, "Ah, gentlemen, I see that you have at last got an instructor suited to your capacities." Other professors taken over by the University of Toronto were Henry Holmes Croft, the Professor of Chemistry, after whom the Croft Chapter House was later named, and the Reverend Robert Murray, a Presbyterian clergyman who had been latterly Professor of Mathematics in King's College. Why some of these were not invited to join the staff of Trinity in 1851, is a matter of speculation. Croft and Murray were probably not acceptable to Bishop Strachan; and the fact that McCaul and Beaven had accepted positions in the University of Toronto in 1850 probably ruled them out when the staff of Trinity was being chosen in 1851. Beaven, in particular, made no secret of the fact that he was not happy in an institution of which he profoundly disapproved. The only reason he continued on the staff of the University of Toronto, and later of University College, was, as he plaintively observed, "that the government has not allowed me any adequate compensation on which to retire, and Providence has not opened to me any other sphere of action." He resigned his chair in 1872, and became rector of the Anglican church in Whitby, Ontario.

With the exception of the Reverend Robert Murray, who died in the spring of 1853, all these professors continued with University College in 1853; and McCaul became, not President of the University, but President of University College. To these

were added a number of new professors. The vacancy created
by the death of the Reverend Robert Murray was filled by the
appointment of J. B. Cherriman, a Fellow of St. John's College,
Cambridge; and four new chairs were created. Daniel (afterwards Sir Daniel) Wilson, a graduate of the University of
Edinburgh, who was destined to succeed McCaul as President
of the College, was appointed Professor of English and History;
Edward J. Chapman, who had been Professor of Mineralogy
in University College, London, became Professor of Geology and
Mineralogy; James Forneri, an Italian veteran of the Napoleonic
wars, was assigned the chair of Modern Languages; and the
Reverend William Hincks, the brother of the Honourable Francis
Hincks, the head of the Hincks-Morin administration, was given
the chair of Natural History. That the appointment of the last
named was an example of the nepotism of the so-called "Reformers" can hardly be doubted; for it is on record that a rival
applicant for the post was Thomas Henry Huxley. He, however,
lacked the qualification of consanguinity with the first minister
of the Crown in Canada, and so continued his career elsewhere.
This was the first, but not the last, time when the effects of the
new principle of "government control" became evident in the
affairs of the College. On the whole, however, it must be confessed that the staff with which University College began its
work in 1853 was not undistinguished.

In the matter of accommodation, however, the College fared
much worse. During its first few years, it was chivvied from
pillar to post. Its first home was the old Parliament Buildings on
Front Street in Toronto, where instruction was given during the
year 1853-54. Then it was announced that the Parliament of
United Canada, which was at this time peripatetic, was returning
to Toronto; and University College was thrust back into the old
King's College building (on the site of the present Parliament
Buildings in Queen's Park), which had been gutted by the Board
of Works. There it carried on for two years. The Government then
decided to take over the old King's College building as a branch
lunatic asylum (which, to add insult to injury, they called the
University Lunatic Asylum); and University College had to take

refuge in a small brick building, later known as Moss Hall, on the site of the present Biological Building of the University. This had been built to house the Medical Faculty of the University in 1850; and for three years, with some temporary additions, it now housed University College, until the present home of the College was completed in 1859.

That University College survived these moves may well be regarded as a miracle. In the first few years, its graduates could be numbered annually on the fingers of one or two hands. In 1855 there was no graduating class at all. During this critical period, when University College was at its weakest, the "outlying colleges," and especially Victoria, continued their attack on the endowment which the University of Toronto and University College had inherited from King's College, and demanded a share of it. This attack culminated in a battle in the Senate of the University in 1863 which I have described elsewhere; it ended, thanks to Edward Blake and Adam Crooks, and other recent graduates, in the defeat of the attack. But the deciding factor in the struggle was probably the advice of John A. Macdonald, who had recommended earlier that the endowment inherited from King's College should be put into the University College building, since (as he sagely observed) not even the opponents of the College could "steal bricks and mortar."

Once University College had a beautiful building of its own (though it housed the offices of the University as well), it began to gather strength. The students of King's College had been drawn largely from Upper Canada College; but the students in University College came mainly from the towns and villages of what is now Ontario, and went back to these towns and villages as country lawyers, country clergymen, country teachers, and country physicians. I have devoted a good deal of research during recent years to trying to track down the graduates of King's College and the early graduates of the University of Toronto (about whom the Records Office of the University had little information), and I make this statement without fear of contradiction. It is clear that, as time went on, University College drew its support from an increasing number of the people of Ontario,

though chiefly still from the Free Church Presbyterians and the
Low Church Anglicans. It might almost be said that Knox
College, and later Wycliffe College, kept University College
alive.

During the period between the completion of the College
building in 1859 and the Federation agreement of 1887, the
College had a steady, if unspectacular, growth. In 1867 the University of Toronto became officially the provincial university of
Ontario; and University College no doubt benefited, as the
teaching department of the University, from this official recognition. The number of students in University College in 1867 was
about 250; by 1887 it had increased to twice that number. During
this period there was no addition to the physical accommodation
provided by the University College building, but there were
some significant additions to the teaching staff of the College.
In 1871 Hincks died, and he was succeeded in the chair of
Natural History, first by Professor H. A. Nicholson, a Scottish
scientist who remained in Toronto only two years, and then by
Professor R. Ramsay Wright, a graduate of the University of
Edinburgh, who became eventually Vice-President of the University of Toronto. In 1872, Beaven resigned from the staff of
the University he had so frankly abominated; and his place was
taken by the Reverend George Paxton Young, one of the legendary figures of University College. In 1876 Cherriman retired,
to become Inspector of Insurance at Ottawa, and his place was
taken by James Loudon, a graduate of 1862, who was destined
to become President of the University. In 1880 Croft retired on
pension, and his chair was filled by William H. Pike, a graduate
of Oxford; and when McCaul retired in the same year, his post
as Professor of Classical Literature went to Maurice Hutton
(later the first Principal of University College), also a graduate
of Oxford. After some hesitation, the Government appointed
Daniel Wilson to succeed McCaul as President of University
College; and he so continued until his death in 1892.

The fact that most of these appointments went to natives of
the British Isles has created the impression that, in its early days,
University College had no native-born Canadians on its staff.

This is far from the truth. In 1856 was appointed the first of a long line of Classical tutors in the College, the Reverend Arthur Wickson, who was a native of Toronto. In 1864, James Loudon, who was born on the site of the present City Hall in Toronto, became tutor in Mathematics; and in 1866 William Henry Van der Smissen, also born in Toronto, became lecturer in German, when the chair in Modern Languages, previously held by Professor Forneri, was replaced by lectureships in Italian, French, and German. In 1876 Alfred Baker, who later became Dean of Arts in the University of Toronto, was appointed tutor in Mathematics, in succession to James Loudon; he too was a native of Toronto. In 1882, W. J. Loudon became demonstrator in Physics; in 1833, John Squair became lecturer in French, and David R. Keys lecturer in English Literature; and all of these were Canadian-born. It is true that, in the early days of University College, the major appointments went to graduates of European universities, and this was perhaps natural and proper; but to say that native-born talent was ignored is far from the truth.

College life had then a formality which it has lost today. Professor J. C. Robertson, who graduated in 1883, has in his unpublished reminiscences (from which he has permitted me to quote), a note illustrating this point. "One feature," he writes, "of all our University examinations was the formal entry at each session of the Presiding Examiner in cap and gown, preceded to the dais by the University Bedel, who bore the University Mace, and who on entering the Hall loudly commanded, 'Gentlemen, stand up!' It should be added that no matriculation student of any Faculty could enter the Examination Hall without a gown. In the Lecture rooms also gowns were very commonly, but not invariably worn. . . . It was still the usual custom in the lecture rooms for students to rise on the entrance of the Professor."

An event which was to bring new strength to the College was the admission of women in 1884. Today the idea of co-education in universities seems so normal that it is difficult to understand the opposition to it in the Victorian era. Yet that opposition was deep-seated. Goldwin Smith, liberal-minded though he was, feared that the president of the College might, if co-education were intro-

duced, have to undertake "the duties of a duenna." Wilson was
in favour of the higher education of women; but he thought that
it ought to be carried out in a women's college, according to the
precedent set by Oxford, Cambridge, and Harvard. However, the
Government of Ontario was not willing to face the cost of establishing such a college. On the other hand, the pressure from the
young ladies who were clamouring for admission to University
College was such that the Honourable (later Sir) George W. Ross,
the Minister of Education, persuaded the Ontario Government to
pass an Order-in-Council admitting women to University College
just as the term of 1884-85 was opening. The resultant problems
created for the authorities of University College in providing
suitable accommodation for women in a building designed for
men (as described by Professor Squair in his pamphlet entitled
*Admission of Women to the University of Toronto and University
College*) are not without their amusing side. Nine women were
admitted to the classes of the College in 1884; but the number of
women steadily increased until at times it has exceeded the
number of men.

It is not necessary to tell here the story of the agreement of 1887,
whereby Victoria University at Cobourg came into federation with
the University of Toronto. That this agreement strengthened the
University of Toronto, since it paved the way for the inclusion of
Trinity College and St. Michael's College as Arts colleges later,
cannot be denied. But for University College it was a serious set-
back. I venture to think that few graduates of University College
now realize that, under the Federation agreement, University
College, which had hitherto taught all the subjects in the Arts
curriculum, was now limited to teaching only those subjects which
Victoria was prepared to teach in 1887. The rest were assigned to
the University, which again became a teaching body. The result
was that while University College continued to teach English,
French, German, Greek, Latin, and Orientals, Italian and Spanish
became "University subjects." Similarly, Modern History became
a "University subject" (apparently in deference to Sir Daniel
Wilson), while Ancient History remained a "College subject."
Philosophy became a "University subject" (perhaps out of regard

for George Paxton Young), but Ethics was assigned to the Colleges. (When St. Michael's became a federated arts college, it undertook to provide instruction in Philosophy, as well as in Ethics; and, of course, it is open to any Federated College to provide instruction in "University subjects" if it wishes to do so.) Later, R.K. (Religious Knowledge) became a "College subject." But Science, Mathematics, Economics, and Law, as well as Italian and Spanish, History, and Philosophy, were assigned to the University. This curtailment of the scope of the College has continued from that day to this. Even when new departments of instruction have been added, such as Slavic Studies, East Asiatic Studies, Psychology, Art and Archaeology, and Business Administration, these have all become "University departments." That the dead hand of the past should have determined this almost immutable division between "College subjects" and "University subjects" may well be regarded as remarkable.

There seems, moreover, to be little doubt that, during the negotiations over federation with Victoria, University College narrowly escaped being turned out of its historic home. Sir Daniel Wilson was the authority for the statement, which he repeated to several people, that it was proposed, in order to meet the objections of the Victoria authorities that they could not afford the expense of erecting new buildings in Toronto, to hand over the University College building to Victoria, and to find "suitable" accommodation for University College elsewhere, probably in the Upper Canada College buildings on King Street. I have elsewhere expressed my doubts about this story, especially as Chancellor Burwash, a man of scrupulous veracity, afterwards denied that he had ever heard of such a proposal; and I find it difficult to believe that politicians of the calibre of George W. Ross and William Mulock could ever have contemplated installing Victoria College in the home of University College. But, as Professor C. B. Sissons has made clear in his admirable *History of Victoria University* (pp. 178-79), there was evidently a proposal by Victoria that "the University work should be carried on in the present main building, and the government should provide other suitable accommodation for U.C." This was a quite different proposal, and might have worked out to the advantage of University College in the long run. But, wherever the truth lies, the removal of University College was thwarted by Sir Daniel Wilson's influence with the Prime Minister of the Province, Sir Oliver Mowat; and the *status quo* was preserved.

The Federation Act, which was proclaimed in 1889 and became effective with the removal of Victoria to Toronto in 1892, brought an access of strength to University College in that it coincided with a number of additions to the staff of the College. In 1888 a professor of Latin was appointed, in the person of William Dale, Professor Hutton retaining the chair of Greek; Professor J. F. McCurdy became Head of the Department of Oriental Languages; H. R. Fairclough (later a distinguished classicist in California) was appointed lecturer in Ancient History, and W. H. Fraser lecturer in Italian and Spanish. The following year Professor W. J. Alexander was appointed to the chair of English, relieving Sir Daniel Wilson of that part of his duties, and William (later Sir William) Ashley was appointed Professor of Political Science. In 1891 G. H. Needler became lecturer in German, J. Home Cameron lecturer in French, and W. S. Milner lecturer in Ancient History. Most of these were Canadian-born graduates of University College.

One might have expected that, once federation was a *fait accompli,* University College could have looked forward to a period of peaceful expansion, side by side with Victoria. But the President of the Immortals (to use Thomas Hardy's phrase) had not completed his sport with University College. Hardly had the Federation Act been proclaimed when the greater part of University College was gutted by fire. On the night of February 14, 1890, preparations were being made for a conversazione of the Literary and Scientific Society of University College. Two of the college servants were carrying a tray of lighted lamps up the stairs in the southeast corner of the building, when one of them stumbled and fell; the ignited kerosene produced a conflagration that spread rapidly; and before the fire was controlled, it had consumed the whole of the east wing, the library of over thirty-three thousand volumes, the museum, and the administrative offices. Only the west part of the building, including the Croft Chapter House, the residence, and the dining-hall, remained intact. The fire was not perhaps such an unmitigated disaster as it appeared to be at first; for, though the loss was not adequately covered by insurance, the Legislature of Ontario came to the relief of the University with a grant that made it possible for the building of University College to rise from its ashes, and the liberality of friends of the University all over the world made it possible to reconstitute the Library of the University and of University College in a separate building, with a book-stock larger and perhaps more serviceable than that which had existed before the fire. But, for the moment, the fire of 1890 seemed for University College a disaster of the greatest magnitude; and it perhaps hastened the death of Sir Daniel Wilson. He died in 1892.

When W. J. Alexander was appointed Professor of English Literature in University College in 1889, Sir Daniel Wilson became Professor of History alone. But History was, under the Federation agreement, a "University subject"; and Sir Daniel then became, though technically President of University College, not a member of the College's teaching staff. Similarly, when he was succeeded by James Loudon in 1892 as President of the University and of University College, Loudon, who was Professor of Physics in the University, was not a member of the teaching staff of the College. The result was that the distinction between the University and University College became blurred, and almost indiscernible.

It is, for example, difficult to decide whether the famous students' strike of 1895 falls into the category of events that belong to the history of the University or of events that belong to the history of University College. It was brought about mainly by students of University College, though the students of Victoria College seem to have acquiesced in it, so far as attendance at lectures in University subjects was concerned; and it was caused by the dismissal of William Dale, the Professor of Latin in University College, and the resignation of F. B. R. Hellems, his assistant, and it ended with the expulsion of R. A. Tucker, the editor of the *Varsity*, who was a student in University College. But it began partly over the appointment of George M. Wrong (later the dean of Canadian historians) as Professor of History in the University in 1894; and most of the complaints of the students were about the administration and instruction in the University, as well as in University College.

I have told the story of the students' strike in my *History of the University of Toronto*; and it is not necessary to repeat it here, especially as it does not seem to have affected greatly the fortunes of the College. It was an episode, and nothing more. I might add that any new light I might now be able to throw on the story relates solely to University politics, and has therefore no place in a sketch of the history of University College. I doubt, moreover, whether the time has even yet come to tell the inside history of the strike of 1895, with all its amazing consequences and repercussions.

One aftermath of the strike I must not omit to mention. In 1895 William Dale was succeeded by John Fletcher as Professor of Latin. (By an amusing interchange, Dale was in the middle of the term of 1895-96 appointed Professor of Latin at Queen's University, the post vacated by Fletcher; but Dale soon returned to his farm near St. Mary's, and there spent the rest of his days.) If the strike brought John Fletcher to Toronto, it did some good, at any rate. He was the first of those Canadian graduates of Balliol College who forged such a strong link between Balliol and Toronto. When I was his pupil, his eyesight was failing; but I owed just as much to him as I did to any other member of the College staff.

University College had become almost indistinguishable from the University of Toronto when, in 1899, the final blow fell. The University College Residence, which had been in operation in the west wing of the College building for forty years, was closed. For this action several reasons were advanced. One was that the Residence was not paying for itself, though it is difficult to understand how a residence that paid no taxes could not have competed with boarding-houses in the neighbourhood that did pay taxes. Another was that there had grown up a rift between the students who lived in residence (about forty in number) and the "outside" students, who lived in Knox College or in boarding-houses, and who numbered in 1899 by far the larger number of students in the College. But the main reason was no doubt the fact that the University, with its growth of staff and students, needed the west wing of University College for purposes other than students' quarters.

About the Old Residence there had sprung up an aura of traditions. One of the most famous of these is the story of the undergraduates who smuggled the steward's cow into the College tower, and tied its tail to the rope of the College bell, with results that startled the midnight air. The son of the steward, the late Mr. J. W. Somers, for many years City Clerk of Toronto, who was living in the College at the time, kindly supplied me with the following account of his recollection of the incident:

> My father mentioned the incident in my hearing several times, and as I was a small boy when it took place, I will give the story as I remember it. I think some of the students in the Residence, which as you know was under the control of my father as steward, thought they would have some fun, so about midnight on Hallowe'en my mother, who was a light sleeper, heard the big bell ring, and roused my father, who was fast asleep. . . . Father got up, and after dressing went to get a couple of the hired men . . . and they proceeded to the tower floor to see who was ringing the bell; and there was one of my father's cows with its tail tied to the bell-rope. The cow was frightened when men appeared and made a mad rush to get away, and the bell commenced to ring. My father held the cow, and the men detached the rope. The next thing was to get the cow downstairs. A cow can be led upstairs, but going down is another thing. It would not start, so it was decided to get some boards and slide it down on its feet, which was successful. The fun was over, and no person was seen during the ceremony.

I had always been sceptical about the story, because I knew that the College gates in those days were closed at nine o'clock, and because I could not see how a cow could have been got up the narrow staircase leading to the top of the College tower. But light broke when Mr. George Kingsford, the son of R. E. Kingsford, brought into my office a drawing done by his father illustrating the incident. This made it clear that the scene was not the main tower of University College, but the belfry outside the old dining-room at the north end of the west wing. The drawing depicted three undergraduates in cap and gown attaching something to the bell-rope in the belfry. It bore the legend "Belles lettres." I am inclined to think that the date on the sketch, "Ash Wednesday, 1869," indicates the date on which the sketch was made, since at that time, according to the records of the Meteorological Bureau, the ground was covered with snow, and that the episode occurred on Hallowe'en, 1868, as Mr. Somers states. The three undergraduates who figured in the drawing would appear to have been R. E. Kingsford (later police magistrate in Toronto), Thomas Langton (who married the daughter of Sir Oliver Mowat), and Isaac McQuesten (afterwards a lawyer in Hamilton, whose son, the late Honourable T. B. McQuesten, stated that his mother had often told him of his father's part in the escapade). There may have been others, but it is clear that the credit for the handy idea of ringing the College dining-room bell by means of the tail of the steward's cow must go to the members of the class of 1869.

Another story is that of the ghost of Ivan Reznikoff, a Russian artisan who had been employed to carve the gargoyles around the College building, and who is said to have been buried at the northeast corner of the quadrangle. Reznikoff's ghost showed itself to various people about the College at different times; and the late Professor W. J. Loudon tells in the fifth volume of his *Studies of Student Life* how on one occasion it visited the room of a student named John Smith, in the Residence. John Smith produced a bottle of Scotch whiskey, and he and the ghost passed a pleasant evening together, which Professor Loudon describes in detail. Then John Smith seems to have suffered a sort of black-out. Perhaps it will be best at this point to quote the statement that Professor Loudon says John Smith gave him:

"The next thing I remember is that I was lying, dressed, on my bed: and, as I looked over at the open window, the sky was all tinged with a golden light, and I realized that another day had come. In fact, I had been asleep. I looked at my watch and found that it had stopped at seven o'clock: then rose, and sat on the edge of the bed for a few minutes, and held my head, as, for the first time in my life, I had a slight headache. Then I stood up and, looking around the room, tried to realize what had taken place the night before. Slowly but surely all the facts which I have already related to you, marshalled themselves, in order, in my mind: until I came to the point where I knew the ghost of Reznikoff had ceased to talk. Then everything became blurred and indistinct. You ask for proof of the presence of the ghost. All I can say is that I know he was in my room, for these reasons. First of all, when I looked about my room, as I tell you, next morning, the fire was not yet out and the shovel, with a kettle, lay upon the coals.

"Secondly, there were two chairs drawn up beside the table and two glasses by the reading lamp (which, by the way, was still burning).

"And, thirdly, on the table, beside the lamp, stood an empty bottle, labelled Loch Katrine, and, beside it, lay a corkscrew and a cork.

"Circumstantial evidence, perhaps, but all I have to give.

"If you appeal to logic and to reason and put aside everything abnormal and bar all psychic phenomena from the evidence, then, of course, all you can infer from the story I have told you is what any judge and jury would undoubtedly decide, namely, *there was a bottle of Highland whiskey, labelled Loch Katrine, drunk in my room, by some person or persons unknown.*

Signed: JOHN SMITH."

I am permitted by Professor T. R. Loudon, the son of Professor W. J. Loudon, to say that his father told him that "John Smith" was a pseudonym for a distinguished graduate of University College, who was later knighted by the Crown.

Still another story is that which relates to the bottle of poison that my friend, the late Eric Armour (afterwards a Justice of the Supreme Court of Ontario and a Governor of the University of Toronto) had in his room. As is well known, alcoholic beverages were latterly forbidden in the Residence; but I am afraid the rule was more honoured in the breach than in the observance. Eric Armour, like John Smith, kept a bottle of whiskey in his room; and, on several occasions, when returning to his room, he found that the bottle had been somewhat depleted. In order to prevent further depredations, he went to the chemist's and bought a black bottle, with a label bearing the skull and cross-bones and the word POISON, into which he poured his whiskey. The next time he came back to his room, he found the black bottle nearly empty, with a note beside it: "Dear Count [his nickname], I have drank your poison, and *crawled away to die.*"

The year 1899 seems to have marked the nadir in the fortunes of University College. With the turn of the century, however, a new era dawned, an era in which University College has gradually assumed the position which it should have been assigned under the Federation agreement of 1887. In 1901 the dining-room of the

College, which had been closed with the Residence in 1899, was perforce re-opened; and under the University Act of 1901, University College at last obtained a principal of its own (as distinct from the president of the University), in the person of Maurice Hutton, of happy memory. Five years later, the College obtained a registrar of its own (as distinct from the registrar of the University), in the person of Professor Malcolm Wallace, who was destined to succeed Maurice Hutton as Principal of University College in 1929. These appointments restored to University College an identity which it had almost lost, and paved the way for the developments of the last half-century.

Since I have now come down to the period with which I am personally familiar, perhaps I may be allowed to record briefly my own recollections of some of those who were added to the staff of University College since that time. Their very names will indicate the calibre of the members of the teaching staff of University College during the past half-century or more.

When I came up to the University in 1902, the staff in Classics consisted, in addition to Hutton, Fletcher, and Milner, of Adam Carruthers (in Greek) and G. W. Johnston (in Latin). Both were conscientious teachers. When Fletcher died in 1917, he was succeeded by John Macnaughton, an almost legendary figure, who had made a mark at Queen's and McGill which unfortunately he did not quite succeed in making at Toronto. When Macnaughton retired in 1925, he was succeeded by Gilbert Norwood, as Professor first of Latin and then of Classics; and in 1951 Norwood, on his retirement, was succeeded by R. J. Getty. A member of the Department of whom perhaps special mention should be made was Oswald Smith, since he was for many years the Registrar of the College. In Ancient History, Milner retired in 1929, and was followed by my old friend, Charles Cochrane, whose premature death in 1945 brought to a close a career of unusual brilliance.

In English, Malcolm Wallace, who joined the staff of the College as a lecturer in 1903, became Head of the Department on Alexander's retirement in 1926; and he in his turn was succeeded in 1944 by A. S. P. Woodhouse, the present Head. In French, John Squair retired in 1916, and his successors were J. Home Cameron and after him in 1926 F. C. A. Jeanneret, the present much-loved Principal of University College. A colourful member of this Department, who joined it as an instructor in 1897, and retired with the rank of professor in 1945, was St. Elme de Champ. In German, W. H. Van der Smissen and G. H. Needler (now Emeritus Professor of German), were followed in 1936 by Barker Fairley, the present Head of the Department. In Oriental Languages, McCurdy had in his later years two distinguished assistants, Richard Davidson (who became Principal of Emmanuel College) and Thomas Eakin (who became Principal of Knox College); but he was ultimately succeeded as Head of the Department by W. R. Taylor, who became Principal of University College in succession first to Malcolm Wallace, and then to Sidney Smith in 1945 (President Smith served for one year as Principal of University College, before succeeding Canon Cody in the presidency of the University). Principal Taylor on his death in 1951 was followed as Head of the Department first by T. J. Meek, and then by F. V. Winnett. I refrain from mentioning other members of the staff of University College who are still living (apart from heads of departments), since the names of these will be found in the Appendix to this volume.

Gradually, since Federation, the University College building has ceased to be known as the Main Building, and has become once again mainly the home of the College. The process whereby this change has been achieved has been slow and piecemeal, and is not yet complete. It was in 1889 that the Department of Biology, with the sub-department of Botany, moved out of University College into the new Biological Building erected on the site of Moss Hall. Later, in 1909, the Botany Department was given a building on the east side of Queen's Park; and finally, it came to rest in its present building on the west side of Queen's Park. In 1894 the Department of Chemistry moved from the Croft Chapter House to the old Chemistry Building, and recently to the Wallberg Memorial Building. Physics left University College in 1907, when the Physics Building was completed (extensive additions have been made to it recently). When Hart House was opened in 1919, the Faculty Union and the Undergraduates

Union, which had occupied part of the Old Residence, were
transferred to Hart House; and in 1923, the offices of the President, the Registrar, the Bursar, and the Superintendent of
Grounds and Buildings, in the University, were transferred to
Simcoe Hall, which became the administrative headquarters of
the University. About the same time, the Department of History,
which had occupied a staircase of the Old Residence, and the
Department of Political Science (including Law), which had
been housed for a year or two in the home on St. George Street
formerly occupied by the President of the University, were all
transferred to the old Cumberland house (now Baldwin House),
at the northeast corner of College and St. George Streets. At the
same time, the Department of Psychology took over the building
vacated by the Department of Political Science, though it continued for many years to maintain a foothold in University
College. Finally, in 1931, the Department of Applied Mathematics
left University College for a house on St. George Street.

It might have seemed that the removal of the administrative
offices of the University and of so many teaching departments
would have left University College in sole and undisputed possession of its own building. But this is not yet true. The University
departments of Mathematics, of Philosophy, and of Italian,
Spanish, and Portuguese, as well as the new Department of Art
and Archaeology, are still housed in University College. University College is not yet a self-contained unit, like Victoria, Trinity,
and St. Michael's; but it is nearer to achieving that ideal.

In other respects, it has gone far toward regaining a collegiate
life. In 1905 Queen's Hall was opened, on the east side of Queen's
Park, in the old Howland house, as a residence for the women of
University College; and this was superseded in 1932 by the
construction of the magnificent residences of Whitney Hall. In
1923 came the Women's Union of University College, on St.
George Street, which was designed to give to the women of the
College some of the advantages that Hart House gave to the
men. In 1924 the old dining-hall was converted into a Junior Common Room for the undergraduates of the College; and in 1925 the
Croft Chapter House was transformed into a sort of Senior Com-

mon Room of the College. In 1932, the College was again given a Reading-Room, in the East Hall of the College, where the Library of the College had been housed before the fire of 1890; and I am glad to think that I had something to do with the opening of that Reading-Room. Now, at last, authority has been granted for the building of a new Men's Residence for University College, replacing the Old Residence abolished over half a century ago.

Pride is one of the seven deadly sins, and it is perhaps sinful to boast even about one's own college. But certain facts may be stated in an objective way. University College has now, and has had for many years, a larger enrolment than that of any other Arts college in the University—a fact that seems to suggest that it appeals to a larger constituency in the country than it did in its earlier days. Where its graduates were once numbered in the hundreds, they are now numbered by the thousands. It is estimated that there are over twelve thousand graduates of the College now living. Of its graduates, one has become Governor-General of Canada, several have become prime ministers, and a great many have achieved distinction in almost every phase of Canadian life. The great majority of the graduates of the College have played, it is true, a humble and unspectacular, though perhaps not unworthy, part in the Canadian community. But no one can deny that University College has, during its hundred years of existence, given a notable contribution toward the making of Canada.

Certainly, it has come a long way since those precarious days of 1853, when it came into being.

G. STEPHEN VICKERS

Building

THE CENTENARY of University College is not precisely that of the building which houses it. In 1853 the College was sheltered in former King's College on the site of the Ontario Parliament Buildings; and it was not until 1856 that the present structure was begun, to be completed three years later. After the humiliation of the previous six years during which it had been housed in a variety of makeshifts, the College moved into adequate quarters for the first and last time in a century. In an effort to spend a handsome endowment before the church colleges could make good their claims to a share, there was erected on a portion of the site set aside in 1828 an edifice of unusual sumptuousness; and, as it turned out, of an unusual style as well. The generations of sightseers who have stared admiringly at the south door of University College while guides have pinned on the label "Norman" could hardly have realized how accidental was the phenomenon at which they wondered. In fact, University College owes its appearance to a tangle of disagreements and concessions, political as well as artistic, the unravelling of which constitutes much of the business of this history.

Writing to his brother in England, the Vice-Chancellor of the University, John Langton, gives the following account of these manoeuvres, involving the architect, Frederic W. Cumberland, the Governor, Sir Edmund Head, and himself.

Cumberland drew a first sketch of a Gothic building, but the Governor would not hear of Gothic and recommended Italian showing us an example

22

of the style, a palazzo at Siena, which, if he were not a Governor-General and has written a book on art, I should call one of the ugliest buildings I ever saw. However, after a week's absence the Governor came back with a new idea, it was to be Byzantine; and between them they concocted a most hideous elevation. After this the Governor was absent on a tour for several weeks, during which we polished away almost all traces of Byzantine and got a hybrid with some features of Norman, of early English, etc., with faint traces of Byzantium and the Italian palazzo, but altogether a not unsightly building, and on his return His Excellency approved.

This is our only description of the creative process; and we might justifiably discard it as caricature aimed to illustrate the meddling ways of high officials were it not such a neat illustration of the stylistic uncertainty and consequent eclecticism of the Victorian Age. The government offices in Whitehall were a comparable field of battle in 1859 with Lord Palmerston, the political power, victorious over Gilbert Scott, the architect. But Head was no Palmerston, and as governor no final arbiter even in matters of taste. It may be assumed moreover, that Langton was using the terminology proper to the 1850's in referring to the suggested styles. He was an M.A. of Cambridge in 1832: as an educated man he would have heard something of the constant antiquarian squabbles over the stylistic divisions of medieval art, especially English medieval art, and must also have read the discussions on the suitability of various styles, ancient, medieval, and modern, when the Houses of Parliament had to be rebuilt after their destruction by fire in 1834.

The architect Cumberland's first choice, Gothic, was no doubt the result of his journey to England and Ireland in the spring of 1856 with the special intention of grounding himself for his commission. There he could see in practice what he must already have studied in illustrations of the leading trade journal of the time, *The Builder*, a "collegiate" Gothic considered especially fitting for educational institutions. It was a patent copy of the late medieval colleges of Oxford and Cambridge, picturesque, casual, and quadrangular in plan. True enough, this modern imitation had become commonplace enough to be used by the Wesleyans; but in the colonies there was a time lag, and only three years earlier Trinity College had completed its new building on Queen Street in a prim and rather archaic version of the collegiate manner.

The Governor's counter, "Italian," is more difficult to interpret, especially as a palazzo in Siena is cited as an example. Ordinarily "Italian" in 1856 would have meant something like the monumental and formal Renascence manner of Osgoode Hall, and would not have been an unprecedented choice for a university building. Many of the Oxford and Cambridge buildings, and the main buildings of the University of Edinburgh, were in the style favoured by the eighteenth and early nineteenth centuries. Conservatives, especially those of a no-popery cast, favoured it; and it was no accident that most of the edifices which grace Whitehall as well as the important clubs were Italian. But there is no model for such a building in Siena, a town which Head, who had written on Italian paintings, knew very well and of whose art he was particularly fond. The "palazzo" *par excellence* of this, the most consistently medieval city in Italy, is the Palazzo Publico, the town hall, built in the fourteenth century, an illustration of which he was most likely to have had in Canada. The deceptive simplicity of a design of great subtlety may have earned the "one of the ugliest buildings I ever saw" from Langton. The Vice-Chancellor's failure to recognize it as "Gothic" is not surprising in one who had come to Canada before Ruskin had made a cult of Italian medieval architecture. Furthermore, it used to be said that Italian art had developed almost directly from Early Christian to Renascence forms: Langton shared, perhaps, this general contempt of what passed in Italy for Gothic.

The check to Cumberland's original conception given by the Italian alternative was not as dismaying, however, as what followed, the Byzantine. To Head, as to his contemporaries, this was best exemplified in San Marco in Venice; it was a style heavy and religious, rich in colour and carvings, and about as adaptable to an educational institution as would have been the Egyptian pyramids. The Governor was playing the traditional role of amateur with a knowledge which outran discretion: it was as well that official business called him away from Toronto to let his enthusiasm cool.

The compromise solution, "Norman and Early English, etc.," today generally described as Romanesque in Normandy and England, was a matter of elimination, that being the only, though hardly the proper, medieval style left. In the history of English architecture this category covers the local variation of a cosmopolitan style which flourished between the Conquest and the early thirteenth century. Of an era before the first universities, it was used primarily by monastic builders whose communities bore something of the character of colleges. The analogy did not present itself to the Victorian mind, however, which thought of this age as dominated by the baronial class, when churches were built by abbots and bishops better qualified to wield sword than crozier, a time of darkness and error best symbolized by the very institution of monasticism. The present writer cannot instance one other example of an earlier or contemporary collegiate institution built in this fashion. The Romanesque had been used for churches during the previous two decades all over Europe and was just coming into fashion in the United States in the years University College was building; but in England at least it had lost ground in the face of Gothic as the architectural style of Christianity. Its more liberal employment by Nonconformist groups indicates that the style was considered more primitively Christian and untainted with ritualism.

In an age which produced a Ruskin to moralize upon every work of art it is difficult to believe that Langton and Cumberland, and all those who accepted the compromise, did not have reasons other and beyond the aesthetic, "a not unsightly building," for their choice of medium. Unprecedented though it was in academic circles, University College could be justified as conforming to nationalist sentiments: it was as English as Ely, or Durham, or Norwich cathedrals. An influential English writer of the day, E. A. Freeman, speaks of the Norman style with its "historical associations which should render it perhaps dearer to us than any other purely Northern creation." At least two of the speakers at the setting of the coping-stone of the College in 1858 struck the patriotic chord. "It [the style] belongs to an old period, coeval with the laying of the foundations of British freedom," said Professor Wilson; and "it is the adaptation of Roman architecture to modern use," in the same manner as Canadian self-government had its origin in Rome, the Governor claimed. The original rationalizations of 1856 are hidden from us; but in the case of a strikingly similar building, the Smithsonian Institution at Washington, we have a whole volume written by the chairman of the board which chose the Romanesque style for the building, in justification of what was for the time, 1849, an equally extraordinary choice. The author, Robert Dale Owen, states that "its entire expression is less ostentatious, and, if political character may be ascribed to Architecture, more republican." A Canadian, especially one who supported University College against both Strachan and Ryerson, might have substituted "less ecclesiastical" for the last phrase of the quotation. There is, apparently, no historical contact between these two rarities, and perhaps no similar justification of the choice of style; but they have this in common—a light indifference to the canons of architectural propriety. We find no such deviations in England.

To return to the text of Langton's letter, the Norman and Early English styles were so well defined in decorative forms, if not in their organic relations, that a skilled draughtsman with a good library could assemble walls having proper doors and windows, towers and apses, all of which could be found in English buildings from the Conquest to 1200. Cumberland was adept at this as indeed was every architect of his time; he had already designed in Toronto St. James Cathedral and the central mass of Osgoode Hall, as dissimilar one from the other as they are each reminiscent of earlier structures. The two stylistic phases suggested by Norman and Early English were not absolutely separable to historians in the 1850's; together they suggested a massive and grand but rather harsh and rude style, in detail softened by graces of Gothic delicacy and naturalism. At the Smithsonian, where the same combination is to be found, the apologist points to the joint purpose of the institution, as a home for the sciences and the arts, respectively symbolized by Norman and Early English. In University College the Early English is pretty much confined to a few carved corbels and capitals in the south tower and the tiny ribbed groin arch in the west entrance. All the rest is not Norman, however, and as surely also is not those "traces of Byzantium and the Italian palazzo" the letter mentions. These latter two artistic condiments are too subtle for the palate of a twentieth-century taster of Victorian fare: perhaps Langton's statements mean only that Head was placated by the retention of some cherished relic of his original suggestions.

The pregnant "etc." includes the other features derived from historical styles. The southeast and east towers and the ramping dwarf blind galleries flanking the south tower are of German origin, and in Toronto an unconscious tribute to the solidarity of the Northern races. The more elaborately carved capitals of the Rotunda, as it is known, and of old Convocation Hall had necessarily to be based on another source than the plastically impoverished Norman English models; and the product is as vaguely reminiscent of a variety of late twelfth-century German models as it is independent of any specific imitation. The chief stonemason was a Bohemian, trained in Austria; but even this explanation is not necessary because German models were well known in British as well as in German publications.

These are not all the elements of the hybrid of which Langton speaks but they are those which the letter mentions. That he evinces no distaste at the process of mixing which went on is no wonder: it is the architectural hallmark of the century in which he was living. That he failed to see other elements is because they either were too deeply buried in his or his contemporaries' tastes to be analysable by him, or at the time when he composed the letter had not come from the hidden resources of the architect.

To speak first of the latter, there is considerable evidence on the extant half-dozen of the originally more than forty-seven plans and elevations, that changes in detail were made after the plans were signed by Langton and Worthington the contractor. These changes are indicated as crude corrections on the drawings and correspond to present appearance; but as old photographs show they had the same form in the building before the fire of 1890. They occurred in the upper levels of the elevation and were aimed to increase picturesque effect or strengthen the composition of the various components of the building. In the main, changes were for the better and in any case minor. One lot of last-minute alterations can be traced to the then Professor of English and History, Daniel Wilson, later President of University College, to whom the south tower owes much of its appearance and all of its effectiveness. An even more radical, and less fortunate, change may have taken place on the roofs of East and West Halls which are now terminated by pavilions as inappropriate artistically as they are anachronistic. There is no extant drawing of the original south face against which to check; but the indications of the south side on the east elevation are of roofs as simple and attractive as those of the east front. Perhaps the introduction of French Renascence *châteaux* roofs for these pavilions was a stylistic subtlety beyond Langton's powers of recognition; but the evidence points to a revision after the letter was sent to England in November 1856.

The purpose of these pavilions is to terminate emphatically the skyline and mass of the southern front of University College, one to each side and in balance with the central tower. There is no medieval equivalent to such an organization: the plan originates in conceptions of geometric symmetry and the "noble front" of the Renascence. Hence the French Renascence effect. Now the basic requirement of composition in a medieval manner was well known to Cumberland and his self-appointed collaborators, an irregular grouping of masses of several shapes, restless and exciting in effect, indefinite and vague in outline, and generally designated in the nineteenth century by the appellation Picturesque. What they did not recognize or were unwilling to admit was the incompatibility of picturesqueness and the commanding front. The *Globe*'s report of the ceremonies in 1858 included a description of the building; and so obsessed was the writer with the symmetry that he supposed all four corners of the central tower were to have turrets only one of which had been finished for the ceremony. The architect and most of his contemporaries could not conceive of a public building, no matter what its function, even an insane asylum, except as a kind of monument to be approached admiringly, its existence appreciated even at a distance, its bulk able to command the avenues and parks which extended around it. As early as the 1840's on a map of Toronto the college site, then at the head of University Avenue, is given larger lettering and a conventional aureole to suggest its importance as Toronto's prime monument. The Governor, who had considerable experience in matters of taste, attempted to rectify this contradiction in style by having the present south face look east across the little ravine; in other words, by giving a quarter turn counter-clockwise to the whole plan. The approach to this regular south front would have been by a winding route through trees and across a shallow ravine, a less formal way than from the south. His suggestion, unfairly described by Langton as sheer wilfulness, would have produced a more consistently picturesque result than now obtains for all sides of the building. The Vice-Chancellor and the architect were more sensitive to the status of the university college as a national institution than an Oxford-trained governor, and quietly turned it round again in the direction it now faces. To the infant institution a bold front was imperative: only ancient, accepted, and privately endowed colleges could turn their backs to the public eye. Theirs was not the immediate victory, however; as long as University College remained the single important structure in the park this south front had little significance. All the old photographs suggest that the normal approach and the most attractive was from what is the Wellesley Street entrance today.

A second architectural solecism is the employment of a conflated church front, comprising the central tower and flanking bays of the south front. To a strict adherent to medieval precedent the result would have seemed monstrous, but the combination has all the spice of improbability without being impossible within the Romanesque idiom, and is a really imaginative solution to a problem precipitated by the Governor's adamant opposition to the Gothic. A Gothic tower can by height gain the prominence in the façade which the Romanesque manner must assert by mass. Cumberland's device obviates the need for an extremely broad and squat tower by equipping the slender member with the two wings whose sloping roofs suggest a church front, back into which the tower has been thrust. Strict adherents to medieval precedent being very rare in Upper Canada in 1856, the solution passed uncriticized. Incidentally, the continuation of the buttresses to the very parapet of the tower, the contribution of Professor Wilson to the elevation, had the same purpose in mind, the strengthening of emphasis on the central tower.

Though Cumberland's original Gothic sketch does not survive we may be fairly sure that it contained a central tower, and a high one at that. Precisely the historical model of the southern front of University College is the Oxford Museum, one of the most notorious monuments of the Gothic Revival. It was to have been a demonstration of Ruskinian idealism; but Oxford was poor soil for so delicate a growth and Ruskin a hasty gardener. At the time of Cumberland's visit in 1856 the blight had not yet settled on the plant, and its architect Woodward, its sponsor Ruskin, and even its sculptors the brothers O'Shea were at the height of their reputations. The main front of the Oxford Museum had a high central tower, equal wings, and over to one side a round structure, the chemistry theatre, removed to a distance to isolate the noxious odours. This was the situation at University College when the present Croft Chapter House served as a physics laboratory and was separated for the same reason from the halls and dwellings of men. But at Oxford science was practised within the Abbot of Glastonbury's kitchen: in Toronto the chapter house of Worcester Cathedral was the pattern. How closely Cumberland followed the Oxford prototype in detail of ornament we cannot tell, for Head's opposition destroyed the surface if not the structure of the building.

To this point the external appearance of University College

has been our entire concern. If this seems an exaggeration of emphasis one can only plead that the preoccupation with the architectural skin was an obsession of the nineteenth century. The interior, aside from the placing of East and West Halls, the residence section, and Croft Chapter House, was apparently left until the outward effect had been more or less settled. Langton tells with what horror the Governor discovered the faculty had need of lecture rooms, the existence of which was finally hidden from him by erasing any indication of desks. The Governor seemingly had in mind a purely tutorial system. It is not surprising, therefore, that none of the lecture rooms or faculty studies is memorable, at least architecturally, and some are very badly designed. Needless to say, they do not conform to a medieval model, whatever that might be. East and West Halls and Convocation Hall which occupied the north end of the east wing were inevitably damaged by the very facility of nineteenth-century carpenters in converting medieval timber-work into a sharp, varnished imitation. Perhaps it is fancy, but the irretrievably lost Convocation Hall seems in photographs to have been the most attractive of the larger rooms, relying chiefly upon a decorative scheme of window framings to unite harmoniously exterior and interior.

It [Convocation Hall] taught us first, the meaning of the builder's art. The great, airy, austere chamber was the most majestic room I have seen in America. The rugged outer wall of grey stone, the smooth and solid inner facings, the tall, clear casements at the sides, whereat green vine-leaves waved in summer, the high-pitched roof with its brown solidity and wealth of grotesque carving—there was one devil with twisted horns, that used to waggle his tongue at me, all through Second Year Mechanics, —the short pillars with every chapter varied, and, more than all, the great painted window above the dais, with its brave, sad story—to learn the meaning of these things, apart and as a whole, was worth at least one place on the Honour List.

Thus wrote a former undergraduate and unwittingly fulfilled Professor Wilson's hope voiced in 1858 "that young minds should especially be developed by constantly gazing on works of gorgeous sculpture and beautiful architecture."

Judged by a contemporary aesthetic the most pleasant sections of the College are the former rooms of the students in residence and the home of the steward at the northwest corner of the plan. Generous and restful in proportions, well-lighted and simply decorated, they have an eighteenth-century air of quiet comfort which no modern residence can show today. No little of the success in this part of the design can be traced to the traditional English plan for college rooms to which Cumberland strictly adhered. The only important medieval flourish in the residence is the cloister: it provides shelter at the expense of sightliness.

This, then, was the building when it was completed in 1859. In it had been combined the legitimate solutions of college housing, the conscious flourishes of ancient styles, the symbolisms of hope and pretension. Vice-Chancellor Langton summed it up when he wrote to his brother, "If asked after the style of our building I may call it the Canadian style." In more fields than the arts it would be difficult to define what "Canadian" meant in 1859: but it was less an indication of refined pedigree than of mongrel vitality.

To the historian of art the subsequent history of University College has much less of interest than the first construction; but there is one peculiarity which has not been mentioned and which for the history of architecture on this continent is worth examination. Presented as a paradox, University College was artistically more contemporary when it was rebuilt after the fire of 1890 than when it was started in 1856. That unwilling pioneer, Cumberland, could hardly appreciate this Hobson's choice; but in working in the Romanesque manner he was handling the one revival style which had a future, though a short one, within the history of modern architecture.

To this day historians of medieval architecture debate the integrity of Romanesque and thereby illustrate its chief virtue as a model to the artistic imagination, the few easily isolated characteristics—the round arch, a quality of massiveness, and a pragmatic rather than a regular solution for each problem of enclosure, cover, and decoration. The round arch is so fundamental a shape that its use is part of the alphabet of design; and combined imaginatively with massive forms produced those expressive masterpieces of brute individualism of the late nineteenth century, the buildings of H. H. Richardson. Only lately it has been demonstrated that the English office and factory blocks of the 1850's and 1860's are the predecessors of Richardson's American work as their inhabitants were the immediate models of the American capitalists. From Richardson to Sullivan to Frank Lloyd Wright is the chain of modern architectural history and the Romanesque stands as a first link of the chain. What England began in the 1860's after a quarter-century of archeological imitation and the United States continued in the 1870's we can hardly expect Cumberland to have anticipated in 1856. He belongs to the last moment of the archaeological phase.

To this point it has been the original University College which has figured in the discussion; but, as many know, the east and over half the south wing were gutted by fire in 1890. The fire did not much damage the walls and external traces of it have vanished. At first sight the present structure is very much like the old; so much like that no novelties of 1890 invalidate the conclusions drawn in the first portion of this essay. The major change was the complete rearrangement of the interior north of the central east door, which had formerly been a Convocation Hall rising through two stories. In order to gain more space for University offices and College staff the handsome and plain hall disappeared, its sole relic today the French Seminar room, once the Senate Chamber, made irrelevantly impressive by the great triple arch in the north wall. The fenestration along the east side was altered in the direction of simplicity and the wooden dormers removed. Along the south front a doorway leading in between Rooms 5 and 11, its corridor now an office, was blocked. One pervasive but not inspired change was the introduction of the gloomy wainscotting in the new section which could well be dispensed with in favour of the plain clean surfaces of the brick walls in the undamaged western part. It was at this time, in 1890, that the elaborately carved door decorations throughout the interior were contrived, many of the devices not very medieval but as carvings infinitely more inventive than the stone sculptures of the 1850's. Two generations of sculptors had been enough to pass from flaccid imitations entirely putty-like in appearance to the bossy fulness of the later decorations. One

of the more happy losses—for fire can clean as well as consume—
was the library in East Hall, a dusty atrocity of Victorian hard-
wood trim: the interiors of both East and West Halls are now
more sentimental than stern, closer to Rossetti than to Scott.

The destruction wrought by the fire was almost great enough
to warrant an even more radical rebuilding, but this was not
suggested. It seems almost incredible that after thirty-one years
of occupancy the building had acquired sanctity enough to
warrant so careful a restoration. The overriding argument in
favour of a more or less exact rebuilding was, as has been
remarked, that the Romanesque was in the 1890's as fashionable
as it had been exceptional in 1856. This was a general American
phenomenon, as visible in Toronto as in any eastern American
city, but particularly apparent at the University itself. Not only
was University College rebuilt but the Biology Building, the
Library, and Burwash Hall were constructed in this fashion.
What is more, this seems to have set the seal upon the Romanesque and its picturesque vagaries for nearly two decades in
public buildings in Toronto: the Parliament Buildings, the City
Hall, and the residential area to the north of the University
known as the Annex, the chief temple of which is the Gooderham
house, bear witness to academic leadership in the past. It is
doubtful whether the prosperous among the citizenry today
would accept a style endorsed by the University.

Since the rebuilding there have been no radical changes in
the external appearances; but the old fabric has been much
mutilated within in an effort to house expanding and temporarily
homeless University activities. It is a sign of the wisdom of the
original builders that a programme, first of getting rid of these
foreign bodies and then of returning the building as far as
possible to its original walls and uses, is indicated. This constitutes no endorsement of antiquarianism: it simply recognizes
the virtues of a work of art however eclectic compared to a
mutilation of it. At the same time, it is hoped that the Norman
myth may slowly vanish so that the true Victorian nature of the
College may be revealed.

MALCOLM WALLACE

Staff, 1853-1890

THERE IS no influence more potent in determining the character of a university than the quality and ideals of the men who were responsible for its establishment. If a university today is still a kind of glorified high school the cause can probably be found in its early history and in the qualifications of its first professors. The close association of Toronto in its beginnings with British universities from which it derived not only the ideal of a university, but a succession of brilliant scholars to illustrate this ideal is a fact of primary importance in the history of our first half-century. During that period men like McCaul, Croft, Wilson, Paxton Young, Loudon, Ramsay Wright, Hutton, Alexander, Baldwin, and Ashley were known throughout the university world for their scholarship, teaching power, and strength of individual character: all of them, in greater or less degree, stamped their influence on Toronto.

Henry Holmes Croft and James Loudon established chemical and physical laboratories which determined the course of University instruction in Science. Ramsay Wright, a graduate of the University of Edinburgh in 1871, joined the College staff in 1874, became Vice-President in 1901, and retired in 1912. For nearly forty years as head of the Biology Department he was regarded by the students in Natural Sciences as probably the most brilliant, and certainly the most persuasive lecturer in the College, and they darkly hinted that his knowledge of foreign languages, including Arabic, was as remarkable as was his profound grasp of the principles of science. If the question of pre-eminence

among the professors had been put to a vote of the student body,
however, a formidable candidate for their suffrage would have
been the Professor of Metaphysics, the redoubtable George
Paxton Young, another graduate of Edinburgh. He and George
Brown, editor of the *Globe,* and William Nelson, head of the
great publishing firm, and Sir Daniel Wilson, President of the
College, had been boys together in the Edinburgh High School,
and afterwards in the University of Edinburgh. Assuredly Professor Young exercised a mighty, if not unique, influence over the
students. One of them, Archibald MacMechan, who afterwards
became the distinguished head of the English Department of
Dalhousie, in succession to Alexander, tells us that Young was "a
survival of an extinct race of giants, the Edinburgh metaphysi-
cians." "His teaching," says MacMechan, "was in effect if not in
method more like what we learn of the teaching of Socrates,
reinforced by the perfervid energy of the Scot. I would not
exchange Young's course in Metaphysics for all the others I took
at Toronto." Another of Young's students, President Patton of
Princeton, says that Young was one of the greatest dialecticians of
the century—whatever that may mean. Perhaps we should remember that we are dealing with a predominantly Presbyterian body
of students, sitting in reverential judgment on a Scotch professor,
and that they were much inclined to use superlatives. Mac-
Mechan, for example, in praising the old Convocation Hall, says
"the great, airy, austere chamber was the most majestic room I
have seen in America." It seems safe at least to conclude that
there were giants in those days. Perhaps fortunately for me, two
of them, Maurice Hutton and W. J. Alexander, are to be treated
by my colleague who deals with the second fifty years of the
College. William Ashley spent only four years in University
College before accepting the chair of Economic History in
Harvard in 1892. In the same year J. M. Baldwin went to Princeton
after three years in Toronto. Both were great scholars, and if we
do not elaborate their services to Toronto it is because there were
more giants than we can deal with in this brief article.

Our first indebtedness was to Trinity College, Dublin. John
McCaul (1807-1886), who for three years of his undergraduate

course concentrated his attention on Mathematics, won the Gold Medal in Classics at the final examination in 1828 when he took his Master's degree. He was appointed University Examiner in Classics, took holy orders, and remained in residence for several years. Almost the whole of his time was devoted to preparing and publishing scholarly studies of Greek and Latin authors. Among these were analyses of the metres of Horace, Terence, and the Greek tragedians. Some of these studies in prosody became text-books in Trinity College and others of the British universities, and spread McCaul's reputation as a classical scholar throughout Europe. Recently, Dr. Stanford, the present Regius Professor of Greek in Dublin, wrote a laudatory review of an unpretentious little volume dated Dublin, 1834, and entitled *Remarks on the Course of Classical Study Pursued in the University of Dublin: Addressed to the Candidates for Honors by John McCaul A.M.* "The general remarks on aims and methods of Classical Study," says Professor Stanford, "are judicious, learned, and as valid today as ever. I have never seen or heard a more succinct or telling address to freshmen, or one better fitted to attract, discipline and encourage them. The subsequent survey of the Honors Course is remarkably sound and able. Whoever troubles to read it now will soon be convinced that the writer was a man of vision as well as of Scholarship."

When John McCaul, then, became Principal of Upper Canada College in 1839 he was a tried and tested veteran in academic matters. He had come out to the New World under the impression that Upper Canada College was in process of becoming a real university, and for a time he seems to have been deeply disappointed. Four years after his arrival, however, that is in 1843, King's College, the charter for which had been secured in 1827, began work as a teaching university. Dr. Strachan was President, and immediately McCaul was appointed Vice-President and Professor of Classics.

It is not strange that the curriculum and scholarly ideals of Trinity College, Dublin, exercised the chief influence in the new college. McCaul's most important colleague, when instruction began, was Professor Croft who had taken his university course at

the University of Berlin and who had been recommended by
Faraday for the chair in Chemistry at Toronto. But a majority of
the staff of King's College had been trained in Dublin. There was
William Hume Blake, the Professor of Law, and Dr. Gwynne,
the Professor of Anatomy. Dr. Sullivan, Professor of Practical
Anatomy, had studied medicine both in Dublin and in London.
Dr. King and Dr. Herrick were graduates of both Dublin and
Edinburgh. When Blake resigned in 1848 he was succeeded by
George Skeffington Connor, another graduate of Dublin, who
afterwards became Chancellor of the University of Toronto. The
little college in the Canadian wilds was directed by men who had
seen men and cities and universities. Both the matriculation
examinations and the prescribed undergraduate course were
criticized as being far too difficult for the great majority of the
high school graduates of the time, and as a matter of fact the
students came almost exclusively from Upper Canada College.
In other words the standards of most Canadian high schools did
not measure up to the standards prescribed in the new college.
This may well have been true, and it is possible that we have
here some failure in practical judgment. But at least there was no
danger that King's College was to be merely a continuation
high school.

Some years later, when the curriculum of King's College had
been taken over by University College, Professor Daniel Wilson
was scornful of this lack of reality in setting standards. He pointed
out that at matriculation a youth was required to have read
Homer's *Iliad*, Xenophon, Lucian, and Virgil, and, if he competed
for a scholarship, to have read all of Homer, the *Iliad* and the
Odyssey both, in fact nearly all the chief classics of ancient times.
No such incredible standard was demanded even in Oxford,
Cambridge, or London. "This," Professor Wilson insisted, "is a
solemn farce." "If our aim is to elevate the education of the whole
province we must provide a matriculation adapted to the specific
capacity of the Grammar Schools." With John McCaul, H. H.
Croft, and Daniel Wilson in control, there was little fear that high
scholarship or practical good sense would be neglected, and after
the establishment of University College in 1853 they modified

the programme they had inherited from King's College. A system of options was introduced after the conclusion of the common first two years, an arrangement made practicable by substituting a four-year Arts course for the three-year course of King's College.

The system of options was explained to the Select Committee of the Legislature in 1860 by Professor Wilson in these words. Our aim, he declared, has been "to devise such a course of study as would prove an effective source not only of intellectual culture but would prepare the youth of Canada for the practical duties of life." "A youth enters our college, and goes through the first two years of the course. He then comes to the President or one of the Professors for advice as to what options he shall take. The matter is very simply dealt with. He is asked—'What is your object in life? If you intend to be a medical man, drop your Latin and Greek and go on with the Natural Sciences and Modern Languages, for every educated man in this country, and especially every medical man, ought to know at least French— which here is a spoken language—and German also.'" Professor Wilson proceeds to explain the advice given to a young man who plans to be a minister, a teacher, a land-surveyor, a farmer, a merchant, or a tradesman, "for," he says, "I trust we are to educate not merely professional men but the youth of Canada generally," and he hopes that students from the farms will multiply every year. It will be noticed, however, that all students take a common two-year course of a cultural kind before exercising their choice of options.

Trinity College, Dublin, and John McCaul left their mark on Toronto in ways which we of today are not accustomed to think of as strictly academic. In other words, McCaul was a cultivated gentleman as well as a scholar, and while performing his duties as President he maintained his interest in many other fields. When the Civil War was raging in the United States, for instance, it was impossible for a Canadian to adopt a neutral attitude. McCaul, like most other Canadians, sympathized warmly with the North and with the emancipation of the slaves. Among the students of University College were some Americans including Southerners, and when a young negro applied for admission to the Literary and Scientific Society the fat was in the fire. President McCaul was successful in bringing the question to a correct solution, for he declared that it would be an infinite disgrace and injury to the College and the University, if any respectable student were denied the privileges of such a representative body on account of the colour of his skin or the blood which flowed in his veins.

McCaul's interests were very wide. The scholarly publications which he had begun to issue in Dublin he continued in Toronto: in the '60's, for example, he brought out his *Britanno-Roman Inscriptions* and *Christian Epitaphs of the First Century*. He founded a monthly magazine, and to it, and to the *Journal of the Royal Canadian Institute*, he contributed articles continually. He was as scholarly and creative in music as in Latin and English, and about 1845 founded the first Philharmonic Society in Toronto. He had a beautiful tenor voice, played various instruments, and published his own musical compositions.

McCaul's most notable colleague in King's College was Henry Holmes Croft (1820-1883), the Professor of Chemistry. Croft's early education was in London where he had been born, and where he attended the Academy in Tavistock House, an excellent school several of the masters of which were graduates of Trinity College, Dublin. On the advice of Faraday, an old friend of his father, young Croft proceeded to Germany where he spent three and a half years at the University of Berlin, at that time the most distinguished school of the natural sciences in the world. Here he won distinction among a group of unusually able students. He studied not only Chemistry but Mineralogy and Geology, Botany, Zoology and Physics, Physiology and Entomology, besides Metaphysics.

Croft shared McCaul's enthusiasm for music, and in Toronto warmly seconded his efforts on behalf of the Philharmonic Society. He was twice President of the Royal Canadian Institute of which he was one of the founders, and to the pages of its *Journal* he contributed many articles. He was also a founder of the Entomological Society of Ontario, which sent a notable exhibit, comprising eighty-six cases, to the Centennial Exhibition in Philadelphia in 1876. All lovers of agriculture and horticulture recognize the debt they owe him especially in his contribution to the establishment of the provincial college of agriculture. His laboratory in University College was built after the style of the Abbot's Kitchen in Glastonbury Abbey—on his suggestion, it is said—and now perpetuates his name in the College as the Croft Chapter House.

Professor Croft's versatility seemed to know no limit. He was the outstanding authority in chemistry in all of Canada, as was fitting, and his researches in toxicology were widely known. For many years he was the Commanding Officer of the University Rifle Corps which owed its existence to his patriotic enthusiasm, and which was in action at Ridgeway during the Fenian Raid when three undergraduates were killed. Professor W. H. Ellis says of Croft that "he was a most delightful companion, steeped with the love of nature, full of dry humour, thinking strongly and speaking fearlessly, but brimming over with kindness." Sir Daniel Wilson's tribute to his old friend is notable: "I have rarely met a man of whom it could be more truly said that in him was no guile. . . . He was most genuinely transparent, honest and straightforward, said and did many unwise things, but never did a mean or ungenerous act. . . . He had set his face very courageously against abuses and stupidities in College management before I reached Canada, and I found myself at one with him from the first in most college matters. I recall him thirty years ago when I landed a stranger in Toronto: young, bright, gay, his wife equally so, both excellent musicians, their house a centre of gaiety, their family a bright young circle."

There are still left a few of the old students of McCaul and Croft who love to sing their praises as scholars, as teachers, and as stimulating, cultivated men. Both were members of the King's College staff throughout its history, and only an impossible constitution prevented it from achieving great things. Both became members of the University College staff when the College was founded, and remained among its chief ornaments throughout. It would be difficult to overstate their influence in determining the character of the College. Both were keen

Churchmen who believed in a non-denominational university. Both had laid a broad foundation in their studies before concentrating on a specialty. Both loved music and poetry. Both were men whose integrity was never called in question. King's College may have had its limitations, but it is well to remember that McCaul and Croft were on its staff from first to last.

When in 1853 University College began its work as the teaching branch of the University of Toronto, Daniel Wilson was the first new professor to be appointed. To the university traditions of Ireland and England those of Scotland were now added, and McCaul, Croft, and Wilson long remained the outstanding members of the staff of the College. Among its early graduates were Edward Blake, Adam Crooks, William Mulock, Thomas Moss, James Loudon, and Glenholme Falconbridge, all of whom were to play an important part in the early history of the University. But the perennial contest between the partisans of denominational and non-denominational education bedevilled the efforts of all these men.

It is difficult for us today to do full justice to these opposing points of view which were defended with perfect sincerity by men who were deeply religious in their personal lives. Even Dr. McCaul in his King's College days defended the constitution of that college, though University College had no more unequivocal defender. Principal Grant of Queen's had entered on his office with a ringing declaration "for one provincial university, amply endowed from provincial resources, its educational interests not sacrificed to the clamours of an endless number of sects and localities," but he was later compelled to side with the sects and localities.

Daniel Wilson's influence on University College was probably more fundamental than that of any other man. When he joined the staff in 1853 he was thirty-seven years of age, and he had already established his reputation in Scotland as a great scholar especially in prehistoric archaeology. Ostensibly, he came to Toronto as Professor of English and History; in reality, his first duties concerned architectural details of the new building of the College, his next the public defence of the ideal of non-denominational education before the Legislature. Dr. McCaul, the President, absorbed as he was in scholarly research, was glad to resign to his new colleague the details of College administration, and it was here, in public advocacy, and in the daily business of dealing with the educational problems of the College, that Wilson was to make his mark. He became a convincing debater, and what was of more importance, he soon developed a sound grasp of educational problems that was unique in the Canada of his time.

A man of profound religious instincts, he never wavered in his conviction that he should, in his own words, "battle for the maintenance of a national system of university education in opposition to sectarian or denominational colleges." When in 1877 he was offered an increased salary to become head of a new denominational college in London, Ontario, he replied very courteously but unequivocally that we must have "untrammeled freedom of scientific and philosophic research. Truth has nothing to fear in the long run from the researches of such men as Darwin and Huxley"; he feared "orthodox zeal" much more. No increase in salary could influence his decision. Wilson had come to identify his own future with that of University College. He had already declined the principalship of McGill, and a cabinet post as Minister of Public Instruction, and when in 1880 he succeeded McCaul as President, he could know no greater ambition.

Wilson's record as President of University College might be regarded as a pretty complete failure if we were to judge by its external events. He believed in university education for women, but in separate colleges. The Legislature decided on co-education because it would cost nothing. He fought the Minister of Education successfully to prevent the disappearance of the College Residence, but several years after his death it was closed. It had been in operation from the time the College opened in 1859, but it was closed effectively, for it has never been re-opened. During most of his régime University College did all of the teaching in the University of Toronto. After Federation in 1889 the bulk of the teaching was handed over to a "University

Professoriate," and the College was continued as a "dwarfed abortion," a "ridiculous simulacrum" to use Wilson's own words. He had sought to hold to the ideal of a non-denominational university, but the new Act subsidized denominational colleges on a most elaborate scale. Wilson comforted himself for all these defeats by emphasizing the fact that the University was now for the first time a truly national institution, and that the prospect for the future was of co-operation rather than of bitter enmity.

But Wilson's abiding influence in the University is to be sought elsewhere. If the Sciences and Mathematics and Philosophy ceased to be part of University College they continued under another name, and Wilson's educational creed had done much to shape their outlook.

What was that creed? Briefly, it was derived from his own experiences in his Edinburgh days, modified by his strong common sense and sound ideals for education in the New World. In the first place he was intensely democratic but he distrusted political legislatures which might know much about how to secure votes, but which were profoundly ignorant of the principles of sound education. Education, Wilson believed, came from significant personal contacts. Good students could do much to educate each other; hence the importance of residences. The mere presence of great scholars on a university staff was a potent educational force; hence, the President's chief function was to secure the services of great scholars, and to remember that the health of the whole nation depended on the fullest development of the highly gifted students. On the second anniversary of the fire in University College Wilson is able in his diary to declare, "We are on the whole, gainers." When there was a danger, however, of losing both Ashley and Baldwin to American universities, he writes, "To lose the two in one year would be worse than the fire." He had been responsible for building up a staff in University College which could compare more than favourably with that of any other American university —in scholarship, in character, and in cultivation. He had established a tradition that a university professor should be not only a great specialist but also a man of cultivated tastes in the

humanities. For many years after his death the staff illustrated
the strength of this tradition in men like I. H. Cameron, Mc-
Murrich, Dean Ellis, H. B. Anderson, J. J. MacKenzie, Primrose,
Coleman, Banting, and McLeod—men whose interest in music
or painting or poetry was as genuine as their scholarly qualifications. We had not yet reached the stage in which achievement in
science and achievement in the humanities were regarded as
mutually exclusive. The only enemy, in Wilson's mind, was
mediocrity. Against it he waged relentless battle as was illustrated by his denunciation of the "nativist" heresy which would
have required that the staff be recruited exclusively from
graduates of the University. In a word, he detested all intrusion
of political considerations in university administration, where
the only legitimate ideal was the enrichment of the institution
by the appointment of great scholars irrespective of where they
had received their training. If he felt little enthusiasm for the
Federation compromise of 1889 it was because he felt that it
ignored purely educational considerations, and was an outcome
of a political point of view. In a word, the firm establishment
of scholarly ideals in Toronto was due to Wilson as much as
to McCaul and Croft. But his acute practical judgment of men
enabled him to surround himself with scholarly colleagues more
effectively than had his predecessors, and his contempt and fear
of mediocrity thrusting itself into the seats of the mighty raised
a powerful barrier against wire-pulling in University appointments.

Wilson preached his educational creed on all appropriate
occasions and especially in his Convocation Addresses. In October 1890, for example, he dealt faithfully with those who even in
the Legislature voiced the opinion that colleges and high schools
were designed solely for a privileged class and not for the people.
"No nation," he declared, "can flourish by a trafficking in knowledge as the mere outfit for professional life." And he concluded
with this unequivocal challenge: "I am persuaded from long
experience that no training is better qualified to fit men for
many practical duties than the persistent diligence of systema-
tized study in any of the departments of university Honour

work." "Our aim in the Faculty of Arts," he added, "is high culture in its truest sense, the pursuit of knowledge for its own sake, and wholly independent of mere professional requirements. But if a result of such training is to secure able and scholarly teachers for our schools, for our bankers men of clearer insight into the principles on which the wealth of nations depends; for lawyers and judges men of cultivated intellect trained in wide fields of philosophic speculation, . . . and for physicians men who have advanced beyond the stage of clinical instruction, and as scientific experts can render a reason for the course that they pursue; this is assuredly a public gain."

What shall we say about these quaint ideas of the later nineteenth century? It is largely an outmoded creed. The aim of the faculty of arts is to achieve high culture in its truest sense, knowledge for its own sake, wholly independent of mere professional requirements! For those planning to enter practical or business life an honours course is deliberately recommended! The chief function of student residences is to make a notable contribution to the intellectual atmosphere of the university! We know that residences are "frills," however useful they may still be as the subject of idealistic public orations. The solution of university problems is really a political question and the blessed word is compromise, not the preservation of intellectual standards. For fifty years we have been told that public money may not be squandered on residences. Education for everyone, able and dull, is our ideal.

It is not to be wondered at that Sir Daniel found himself isolated in the Federation discussions. The distinction between "College subjects," and "University subjects" was not made on any educational theory. University College was to teach only such subjects as Victoria College found it convenient for her to teach. Accordingly, French and German found themselves in the Colleges, Italian and Spanish in the University, Ethics and Ancient History in the Colleges, Philosophy and all other kinds of History in the University. To Sir Daniel this seemed treason to all serious university standards. Moreover, the plan to relieve the students of Victoria and any other denominational colleges from all payment of University fees he recognized as a revival of the old demand for denominational endowment. To him this subsidizing of denominational colleges by the state was unique among the universities of the world, and indefensible.

If Sir Daniel never pretended to much enthusiasm for the solution, the members of his staff felt even less. Long years after Sir Daniel's death the Council of University College in the brief which they submitted to the University Commission of 1906 deplore the cleavage between the two parts of the state Faculty of Arts, which they describe as wholly artificial and caused by circumstances outside the Faculty itself. It had, they say, introduced needless obstacles in the way of common and efficient action, and in the so-called College subjects a rigid and cumbrous system which hampers the work in these subjects, fetters individuality, and prevents the development of the curriculum and freedom in methods of instruction. They recommend that the state Faculty of Arts be reunited, and that the Arts Faculties of the Federated Universities be incorporated with and become part of the state Arts Faculty, the fees for instruction in Arts being then payable to the University. The Senate of Victoria College, on the other hand, said that in their judgment it is not in the interest of the University, or of the Colleges, or of the country, that any serious change should be made in the general plan or ideal of the University. Both parties understood perfectly that the struggle was the same struggle which had been waged for half a century, namely the demand for a division of the University endowment between the University and the denominational Colleges.

In other words, the victors were satisfied with their victory, and the losers could only register their protest. Victoria had secured her share of the University endowment in the shape of freedom from fees. She continued to teach the subjects which she wished to teach, took an important part in the government of the University, and when she looked back on her Cobourg days was not inclined to regard her present status as that of a ridiculous simulacrum.

And yet it must be confessed that Federation has been a fairly successful experiment. It has broken up the huge student body, and provided living accommodation for many students. That Toronto maintains four separate departments of Greek and Latin, of Oriental Languages, of Ethics, and of Ancient History, does not seem to trouble anyone particularly, since the important subjects like Sciences and Economics are spared. Now University College is about to have a Residence for men as the other Colleges have had for more than half a century. Sir Daniel consoled himself with reflecting that at long last there was a prospect of a really great national university. In his own words: "I have resolutely battled for the maintenance of a national system of university education in opposition to sectarian or denominational colleges. In this I have been successful, and I regard it as the great work of my life." It is surprising how much comfort rational men can extract from reflecting that questionable developments were written in the stars. One finds it difficult to believe, however, that the present situation will be permanent, for its anomalies grow more rather than less objectionable. For instance, to maintain the existing system, the fees in Arts have been repeatedly increased, and two-thirds of these fees go to the federated Colleges instead of into the University treasury.

One last word about Sir Daniel. He was criticized for holding an aristocratic ideal of university education, and there was superficial truth in the charge. He regarded the gifted student as the chief asset of the university, and the maintenance of intellectual standards as its fundamental ideal. He detested a democracy which insisted that Jack was as good as his master, irrespective of the tastes and interests of both. Sir Daniel's thinking on educational subjects was original, not derivative, and it was conditioned by his integrity, his penetrating common sense, his unequivocal devotion to high ideals, his great intelligence, and his generous instincts. The political well-being of Canada absorbed his attention even as he worked for her intellectual health. The business of the university was to produce a steady supply of men capable of elevating the public conception of business and of the professions—"leaders of the people by their counsels and by their knowledge of learning meet for the people"—for he believed profoundly that the health of the community depended on such leadership. His original common sense was seen in his insistence that French and German options should supplement a purely classical training. He feared the organizations that had become an end in themselves, and warned his fellows against the limitations of a department of education which prescribed uniformity of text-books and examinations. "It leaves no room," he declared, "for the men on whom the reputation of universities has ever most largely depended, and no time for the wider range of spontaneous and suggestive illustration best calculated to stimulate the enthusiasm of the gifted student." "The more latitude," he concluded, "that a thoroughly qualified teacher enjoys, the greater will be his success in all but routine work."

The inherent wisdom of these convictions will always make its appeal to serious students of education. To Sir Daniel the enemy was routine and uniformity, and subordinating real education to the practical purpose of making a living, instead of concentrating on the development of the gifted student. He would make the ultimate test of any system of education not examination results but the kind of men and women it produces, and the interests and ideals it implants.

It is obvious that Sir Daniel never forgot the educational ideals of the Edinburgh to which he owed his own early training. We cannot take leave of him more appropriately than in the words of one of his old students who was also his biographer and close friend, Mr. H. H. Langton. "Upon those who were brought closely in contact with him in everyday life, his considerate courtesy and genuine goodness made a deeper impression than even his intellectual gifts and his ability in practical affairs. The memory that Sir Daniel Wilson has left behind him with those who knew him best is one that great men might envy—to be reverenced and loved for what he was, even more than to be admired for what he did."

This proud estimate by one of Sir Daniel's old students, who is also one of our wisest and most scholarly graduates, I commend to those who are now responsible for shaping our educational policy and for preserving the reputation of our wisest benefactors. More than any other name in our century-old story that of Sir Daniel is honourably associated with faith in residences as educational instruments, and with a conception of education which refuses to debase standards at the behest of the multitudes, or to let go the old ideal of producing men and women of outstanding character and ability—"leaders of the people by their counsels, and by their knowledge of learning meet for the people."

A. S. P. WOODHOUSE

Staff, 1890-1953

AS ANOTHER CHRONICLER takes up the subject of the Staff after Federation, he may be permitted to state the conditions of his task and the method by which he will proceed.

In this period, 1890 to the present, the range of the College's teaching has been reduced to six subjects in the Humanities: Classics (including Greek and Roman history), Semitics, English, French, German, and Ethics; and all other subjects have been relegated to the University. In these six disciplines alone, then, we must seek our notable figures. Two problems immediately appear. What shall be our criteria of selection? And, since influence on the course of liberal education in the University must clearly be one, and we would avoid even the appearance of exaggeration, how can we differentiate sufficiently sharply between the effect of University College, with its notables, and that of the Colleges joined with it in the Federation?

Some answer to this second question is supplied by a series of converging facts: by the position of University College as *primum inter paria* in the system, especially emphatic in the first thirty-five years of our period; by the simple series of dates at which the constituent Colleges entered the Federation, Victoria (1890), Trinity (1904), St. Michael's (1910); by the crucial case of the honour course in Classics, which assumed its main outlines in the decade between 1880 and 1890, and which has in large measure established the philosophy and set the pace for all the rest, and by the evident connection between the

outlook and ideas of the notables and the educational aims and
methods which the Federation has pursued.

The first question—the criteria for selecting the figures to be
treated—presents more difficulty. The number of men perman-
ently connected with the College who have made no contribution
to it has been fortunately very small. Yet, if the essay is not to
become a mere catalogue, there must be rigorous selection and
on a principle clearly defined. Here then is the principle. Of the
figures who spring instantly to mind (when one has eliminated
all names at present on the active roll of the College), some few
have achieved a high place and an international reputation in
scholarship or criticism; two or three others, without publication
sufficiently extensive or so placed as to obtain international
recognition, have still produced work of the highest quality; and
finally there is the larger group who, with or without published
work to their credit, and whether or not they may claim a place
in either of the former categories, made the deepest impression
upon successive generations of students, enjoyed a unique reputation within the University, and left their indelible stamp on
the teaching of their subjects. In this last class a pre-eminent
example would be Hutton, whose writing, for all its urbanity,
is not of the highest order or a fair measure of his power, but
who shaped the honour course in Classics and impressed and
charmed every audience that came under his spell, or Alexander,
whose writings clearly place him also in our second category,
but whose unrivalled influence upon his students, and upon
the teaching of English both in the University and beyond it, are
far more widely recognized, or Brett, whose contributions to
Philosophy assign him to our first category, but who also deserves
an honoured place in the third. These merely by way of example;
from what will be said of the other figures selected it will not
be difficult to determine why one regards them as notables or
in which of the categories they fall.

Alumni, reading this essay, will doubtless recall with gratitude
or affection many another figure: in Classics, for example,
Fletcher, Macnaughton, and Oswald Smith; in French, Squair
(of the famous *Grammar*, which achieved its own international

reputation and must be briefly mentioned below), de Champ (who did much for the teaching of the spoken language and in his own person introduced us to the Gallic spirit), Cameron (with work in composition) and McKellar (with work in phonetics); in German, Van der Smissen, and Needler (whose translation of the *Nibelungenlied* won immediate recognition, and whose retirement launched him upon a new career of research in his favourite English writers, always with some German or some Canadian connection); in Ethics, Tracy; and in English, Keys, Clawson, and Macdonald. Around some of them sprang up that luxuriant growth of anecdote which no college worthy of the name should be without—the story, for instance, which De Lury loved to tell, of Squair's desire to familiarize his students with the glories of French art, of his wholesale import of reproductions, which he and his colleagues industriously hung in every classroom, of the irate protest of Baker, who demanded their instant eviction as too apt to distract attention from the more austere beauties of Analytical Geometry, of their hasty removal to Squair's office, there to confront the horrified gaze of Mrs. Jones (from somewhere out in the Province) who had called to inquire how Mary was getting on with her French. Or, again, a whole series of stories about Keys, the most gregarious, as well as the most absent-minded of academics, who hurried from one engagement to another and arrived—if nothing occurred to distract his attention on the way: "I never think of him," said one colleague, "without remembering the text, 'Where two or three are gathered together, there am I in the midst' "; and at the dinner given in his honour upon retirement, did not the good man himself pull out his watch and exclaim, "There is another meeting I ought to be attending at this moment"? Or finally stories of another sort, recording the ready answer, as when a student, disappointed with a mark of 64, was so rash as to protest, "There's something wrong here, sir, you gave this same essay 67 last year": "Ah," said Macdonald, "you are not allowing for depreciation."

But to return to the names selected for discussion as falling into one or more of the three categories suggested above: there are perhaps a round dozen, a number, and of a quality, hardly to be matched in this limited range of disciplines, and in the same period, by any other academic body in Canada. We may try for a degree of significant coherence in our account by grouping them in disciplines, by proceeding chronologically within each discipline, and by relating their effort to the work of the College as an institution of higher learning.

In the decade before Federation commenced, honour Classics, as it still exists, was securely established and on its way to widespread influence and continental fame. The strength of the tradition is attested by the fact that in the general retreat from the Classics which has impoverished North America they held their own at Toronto longer perhaps than anywhere else. And that tradition was pre-eminently the work of Maurice Hutton and the men whom he trained. On his retirement some of them joined to record the debt to him, in *Honour Classics in the University of Toronto* (1929). Of the course they wrote: "Others . . . have helped in its building, but its beginnings it owes to the new life which he brought with him, and its development largely to his rich and generous personality." Under his predecessor, John McCaul, an honour course in Classics had indeed existed, with formidable reading requirements, but with attention falling upon expression rather than content, with little concern for history and philosophy, and with no very coherent principle of organization. All this Hutton gradually changed. Under his direction honour Classics became a Canadian adaptation of Oxford "Greats," with some concession to the inferior training in the two languages with which the students came up, but with the clear determination that they should graduate possessing an adequate command of both and having reaped the benefit of a study, intensive and extensive, not only of classical literature, but of ancient philosophy and of Greek and Roman history. The great works of antiquity were read for their content as well as for their language and style. Texts of Plato and Aristotle furnished the basis of a critical and historical study of Greek thought, and the texts of the ancient historians furnished the starting point in Greek and Roman history. Thus literature in its widest definition dominated the course, and it is significant that in reading the philosophical texts much less attention, we are told, was paid to "metaphysics and epistemology" than to the "moral and political ideas" which they contained.

Here, then, is a striking example of the way in which University College, through the work and influence of Hutton, gave direction to the aims and methods of the Arts course at the honour level. For honour Classics, as we have observed, furnished a model and set the pace for other honour courses in the Humanities. The special marks of these honour courses at Toronto are: the selection of a sufficiently important and productive area of concentration—the Classics, it may be, or the ancient Semitic world, or English, or two of the other languages of modern Europe—an area with its own internal relations and its recognizable contribution to life today; the systematic exploration of this area as supplying the principal content and the focus of a four-year course; the insistence on the command of texts as the basis of the whole effort—the reading of the books themselves, not the acquisition of mere information about them; the generous conception of literature, which extends beyond *belles-lettres* to include the literature of ideas, but studied always as literature addressed to the general reader; the placing of these texts in their historical setting, with the result of illuminating the texts and of gradually giving to the student such command of the history of his area as no series of survey courses ever achieved, and finally, as the outcome of it all, possession not only of a considerable body of the world's best knowledge, but of a habit of mind and a point of view which might also be a starting point for further exploration. Classics was the first course effectively to demonstrate in Canada the grand aim of the honour system, general education by means of judicious specialization. But the description attempted above will apply, *mutatis mutandis,* to all the rest.

Not upon honour Classics alone, but upon his students, Hutton exercised an abiding influence. One of them, recalling him and his principal colleague of early days, wrote:

If ever there was an ancient Roman, it was William Dale; if ever there was a Greek born out of due time, it was Maurice Hutton. Dale was austere, . . . methodical, concise, meticulously accurate himself and critical of anything short of complete accuracy in others. . . . Hutton was a brilliant Periclean Greek, far-ranging, witty, gently sarcastic, but with the ever-present understanding and tolerance that go with broad culture: an illuminating expositor, an incisive critic, constantly clinching . . . a fact or an idea by . . . an illustration or parallel drawn from his wide knowledge of history and literature. . . . He was an erudite and urbane Plato with a dash of the lightheartedness of Alcibiades. . . . He made us feel that the classics are not dead, but vital, active, modern, and still permeating life and thought.

Much of this portrait one can confirm from Hutton's writings —but not all. Evidently, the Roman spirit grew upon him with advancing years. His weightiest effort, *The Greek Point of View,* exhibits the ranging mind, the flair for historical and contemporary parallels, and a suggestive study of language as indicative of idea and attitude, the qualities which made Hutton so effective as a teacher; but it also gives unmistakable evidence of a feeling, amounting almost to hostility, that the Greek point of view had profound limitations and inadequacies, that it was too intellectual, too analytical, too much prone to dismiss whatever could not be clearly and cogently formulated in words, too little concerned with faith and conduct and with their parent, the will.

This is perhaps understandable, and first in terms of Hutton's own period and background. The limitations emphasized are those implied by Arnold in his definition of Hellenism and not unrecognized by Pater. With these two critics the essential contrast is between the Greek and the Christian. With Hutton the overt contrast is between Greece and Rome—the Rome of republican simplicity, unsophisticated thinking, and traditional virtue, with whatever of this legacy passed to the rulers of the Empire, so that one is tempted to say that among Grecians Hutton was the noblest Roman of them all. But his attitude, which he perhaps never paused to analyse completely, is not so simple as that. The contrast of the Greek and the Christian lurks just below the surface and at times emerges; and the matter is further complicated at a shallower level by a suspicion that the Greeks were "too clever by half" and at times departed rather violently from the standards of an English gentleman.

Significantly, he observes, they used the same word (λόγος) to denote reason and speech: nothing was a reason, which could not be put into words. Thus they were driven back—or, rather, willingly retired—upon partial explanations. With all their penetration and their eloquence they could find no better motive and sanction for patriotism and the civic virtues than enlightened self-interest. Hutton dissents from Bradley's assertion that "with every step in the socialization of morals and the moralization of politics, something of Greek excellence has been won back." No doubt Aristotle described ethics as a branch of politics (that is, of the conduct of society), but the description depletes ethics quite as much as it enriches politics. And, anyway, for the Greeks the virtues, whether private or political, were

the achievements of a clear brain and not of a disciplined will or of an instinct that is active. . . . But this distinction of knowledge and will, this preponderance of intellect in the Greek system of ethics, and this minimizing or ignoring of the will, is the very heart and core of all that is most characteristic of Greece both in theory and practice, and most alien to later civilization, whether Roman or Christian.

Dangerously inadequate in the sphere of politics, the Greek point of view offered, he held, even smaller basis for the private virtues. It is true that Plato, "least Greek of all Greeks," talks of "the man within" and of "a mysterious relation who shares his house and acts as keeper of his intellectual conscience"; but this is far from embodying a full conception of the inner life, and there is "a gulf between the self-examination of Socrates, convinced of ignorance, and the self-examination of the Christian, convinced of sin." The "processes of the religious life have their Platonic and Socratic parallels, but the parallels run far apart: the Greek experience lies always in the world of intellect as the experience of the religious mind lies in the world of emotion and of character."

In reality the contrast of the Greek and the Christian emerges as for Hutton more significant than the others which he draws or suggests. It was Christianity which most clearly recognized the importance of the will and of the inner life. Since Hutton's day scholarship and criticism have tended increasingly to emphasize the harmony of the classical and Christian outlooks and the

ease with which a synthesis was effected in the Christian human-
ism of the Middle Ages and the Renascence; but it is altogether
possible that the swing of the pendulum has gone too far, to the
obscuring of some fundamental differences in the two outlooks
and of the recurrent tensions between them. Against such an
error Hutton's analysis, incomplete though it be, is a useful
antidote.

At the same time one should remember that the Christian
tradition is quite as complex as the classical, and that Hutton's
exalting of the will at the expense of the reason plainly aligns
him with the voluntarist wing of Christian thought and leads to
a degree of obscurantism and even primitivism. If, says Hutton,

a Greek or a Greek-minded modern tell us that virtue is knowledge, what
can one more usefully retort than that the bald opposite is as true? that
virtue is ignorance and that ignorance is bliss . . . , that ignorance, which
the Greek describes as vice, is as often innocence . . . , modesty, faith,
hope and charity, or again true passion and idealized desire—a whole
catalogue . . . of virtues and . . . the truest wisdom? For every man who
has achieved . . . virtue . . . by hard thought, it is easy to find some one,
some nation even, like the early Romans, who were very virtuous and
very ignorant, whose virtues disappeared with their ignorance, whose
vices began with their Greek philosophy. . . .

To Hutton Socrates seems like a premonition of the Master of
Balliol, both of them "terribly at ease in Sion"; and the Carlylean
phrase is perhaps another clue. Hutton's judgment of the Greeks
is not uncoloured by fitful lights from nineteenth-century Roman-
ticism—its exalting of the primitive, its preference of doing to
thinking, its depreciation of reason—or by a strong reaction
against Victorian rationalism. Jowett and Mark Pattison (as his
essay on "Some Oxford Types," in *Many Minds*, confirms) were
not among the gods of Hutton's idolatry: he preferred the aged,
pious, lovable, slightly ridiculous, and now forgotten Provost of
Worcester. The Greeks (as another of the essays in *Many Minds*
confirms) seemed to him too much like Frenchmen or even
Shavian Irishmen: it was the solid, active, practically pious
Romans who foreshadowed God's Englishmen, their successors
in empire; and here perhaps is another clue. Though the English
universities aimed at an all-round training under the comprehen-

sive formula, the education of a Christian English gentleman, Hutton felt that in the Oxford of his memories the Greek exalting of the intellect too much prevailed. Only there and in Athens, he remarks, would one meet the confusion of goodness with intellectual endowment or attainment; and Athens, he added, was not so much a state as a university!

The Greek Point of View was committed to print in its author's elder years and perhaps bears too deeply their impress; but Hutton's point of view undoubtedly sharpens his perception of certain aspects of the Greek mind. Reading the book helps us to understand his acknowledged effectiveness as a teacher and as a stimulus of youthful thought, just as the collected essays help us to understand his success as a popular lecturer and a missioner of culture to the Province. With Jowett he agreed at least in this, that the business of the university professor was education, not research; and he quotes with relish Jowett's comment on Bentley's boast that he had read all the commentators: "Then he kept very poor company." Professor J. C. Robertson reports that Gildersleeve thought Hutton's work interesting, "but not exhaustive"; later Hutton visited Johns Hopkins and, addressing Gildersleeve's seminar, "delighted them all." There is perhaps something artificial about a situation in which research and education confront each other across a dizzy chasm. The middle term is lacking, which might bridge the chasm: that term is *productive scholarship*, and scholarship can produce men as well as books. Of men Hutton's productive scholarship bore a goodly harvest.

W. S. Milner, who graduated in the year after Hutton's appointment, seems to have been in complete agreement with him in the general conception of education and of the honour course, but Milner had his own outlook and the more philosophical mind; also, Milner was by birth and training what Hutton never, by adoption, really became, a Canadian. It is significant that sharing (as did that other sterling product of University College, William Dale) all Hutton's enthusiasm for "Greats," he nevertheless describes the Toronto honour course, not as an adaptation, but as an independent effort directed to a similar end. Like Hutton's, Milner's interest centred much on ethics and politics, and on the application of the principles of Greek thought beyond its immediate period and frame of reference; but since he was deeply versed in the history of political theory, his excursions became in effect an introduction to the whole subject.

By no ordinary standards could Milner be described as a good teacher. He had, for example, nothing of Alexander's unfailing lucidity and cogency or of Brett's system and precision. He was saturated in his authors and in the inferences which he had drawn from them, but one could never foretell what the precipitate from all this erudition and philosophical contemplation would be on any particular day. In his seminars he would read a few lines of the text and commence thinking aloud. Often he appeared to reach no conclusion. "We'll hang that up," he would drawl, when the thoughts ceased to flow and it became necessary to resort to the text for a new starting point. No one ever knew him to take down and resume any of the unanswered questions which seemed to festoon the walls of the seminar room. They had served their purpose: the process was the end. But long before the course finished there had emerged a body of principles which one might wish to modify but could never forget.

Milner's seminar on the *Politics* sometimes commenced with an affirmation, delivered in a monotone and with his gaze fixed abstractedly on the upper right-hand corner of the door: "Aristotle had the greatest—possibly not the finest, but certainly the greatest—intellect with which man was ever endowed." The parenthesis was to make sure that he was not being unfair to Plato; but we were left in no doubt that Milner was born an Aristotelian. The Greek point of view, at least as manifested in Aristotle, he could accept with far fewer reservations than could Hutton, partly because his religious thought and feeling were not of a kind to breed tensions with it. In his discourses there were strong intimations of natural religion, and he emphasized whatever in Aristotle's view of nature and man seemed to confirm them: man was by nature a political animal; nature did nothing in vain; it was not for nothing that human experience demanded insistently such and such an inference; the end was the chief thing of all; and the Aristotelian teleology could be grounded finally only in natural theology. Nature must mean, he would say, "God in the world." Perhaps this was a rather larger—at least a more unqualified—conclusion than some expositors would draw from the text of the Philosopher; but it was evidently in line with that great Aristotelian, Edmund Burke, with whose habit of thought Milner was in profound sympathy. For like Burke he coupled with a basic theological assumption an astonishing realism in dealing with men and their ways in political society, and within the limits of his essential conservatism manifested an open and flexible mind.

Like most of his contemporaries, Milner was an educator rather than a writer. Indeed he wrote very little, and nothing that exhibits his full quality; but his chapter on "The Higher Life in Canada," contributed to *Canada and Its Provinces,* is as characteristic of him as it is unlike other contributions. More than half the chapter is devoted to education, with emphasis upon the honour course as the means of fostering quality in a society whose note is equality (a problem which also engaged Hutton's attention). Milner, it is clear, is committed to democracy, and to North American democracy, but (as he hopes) of a distinctively Canadian type which will carry with it an adaptation of historical institutions and a sense of obligation to offset the insistence on democratic rights—a type, in other words, that would pass muster with an Aristotle or a Burke. Of the hazards of the North American experiment he is well aware, and on disquieting manifestations south of the Border he keeps a vigilant but never unsympathetic eye. There are problems to be faced, but also solutions available; and he has a large underlying confidence in "the first two axioms of politics: that men are actuated by the same motives, and that they would not form into societies if they were not capable of working together." In other words, man is a political animal, and nature does nothing in vain.

C. N. Cochrane was taught by Hutton and Milner, and succeeded the latter in the chair of Ancient History. He was in this

degree typical of the next generation of scholars: abating nothing
of his belief in the scholar as educator and the virtues of the
honour course, he also felt the impulse to communicate with a
larger audience by the printed word. Thus he took his place, and
helped his University and College to take their places, in the
republic of letters. To make clear the significance of his two
principal books, I must beg leave to adapt some paragraphs
which I wrote for the Royal Society of Canada at the time of
his death.

In *Thucydides and the Science of History* (1929), Cochrane
contends that the historian did not lack, as is often supposed,
"scientific categories" and "the conception of law as applying
to human actions." These he shared with the Hippocratics, the
exponents of the positive science of ancient medicine, whose
meticulous record of case histories is the closest analogue of his
method in the *History* as he deals with the character of peoples,
the genesis and fortunes of states, and the motives of individuals.
His attitude was strictly scientific: it was not mythological as
relying on supernatural intervention, nor was it (like so much of
later Greek thought) metaphysical as presupposing a set of ideal
values to which human life, if it was to have any significance,
must be somehow made to conform. The true antithesis to
Plato, says Cochrane, is not Aristotle but Thucydides. He escaped
the fatal dichotomy of mind and matter, and with it the illusions
of the idealist and the materialist. For he concerned himself with
what was, not with what ought to be; and, though he started
with the physical, he did not stop there, but viewed the human
being as a living whole whose environment was customary and
institutional as well as physical, and he was thus under no
temptation to reduce the laws of human action to mere mechan-
ism. In Thucydides history depended upon, indeed itself
approximated to, a broad and realistic conception of political
science. Near the end of the book there is a significant remark:
the true successor of Thucydides was St. Augustine. It was
destined to become the starting point of a far more extended
effort, *Christianity and Classical Culture: A Study of Thought
and Action from Augustus to Augustine* (1940).

The ground common to St. Augustine and Thucydides was their realism: their firm hold on verifiable human experience as yielding the law of man's actions, their refusal to break up this experience and sacrifice a part of it for the sake of an explanation, either idealist or materialist, as was the manner of many other thinkers. But St. Augustine went beyond his predecessor in the range of experience considered, and in another way. In Thucydides it is proper to speak of a science of history, but not of a philosophy of history since of the historical process no end is envisaged. In St. Augustine the science of history, brought into conjunction with Christianity, issues in a philosophy of history. What others sacrificed the science to obtain (and failed of obtaining) St. Augustine achieved with no such sacrifice. He could do so because he had discovered a sound theoretic basis. For the partial and inadequate principles invoked by ancient philosophy, whether idealist or materialist, he substituted "the *logos* of Christ," the foundation of *nostra philosophia*. Here the problems which had exercised the classical mind received their solution or were shown to be meaningless. Instead of the different principles advanced by the philosophers, there was one Principle, God, the source of being and of goodness, of order and of every other true value which philosophy had known. The mode of their diffusion (another problem) was creation *ex nihilo*. Evil (again a problem) was to be explained neither as principle nor as attribute of matter, but as mere deprivation. As God was Creator, so man was a creature, composed of body and soul (both real, i.e., neither of them illusory or a mere function of the other); and as creature he was dependent on his Maker for all his well-being, corporal and spiritual, temporal and eternal, and for the values embraced by such well-being and necessary to its attainment and enjoyment, values verifiable in experience but receiving their adequate sanction (for which philosophy had inquired in vain) from the command of God. The creature was bidden to be perfect, and the perfectibility which philosophy had declared to depend on his own effort (or alternatively had despaired of) was exemplified in the Incarnate Christ and implemented by grace. It depended not upon knowledge merely (as

philosophy had supposed) but also upon will and love. If, though
perfectible, man and society were indeed imperfect, the explanation was the Fall, and the remedy was the scheme of Redemption
and the gift of grace for all who would receive it. Those who did
were the *civitas Dei*, the perfect society committed to all the true
virtues, individual and social, which philosophy had ever
glimpsed, and more, because committed to the love and service
of God; the rest, who served not God but themselves, were the
civitas terrena, which none the less owed whatever it possessed
to the Maker. In terms of these two cities St. Augustine viewed
history, over whose course the Providence of God presided. The
view taken of history is itself, Cochrane held, an historical fact
of the first importance in any period. The conflicting views
classical and Christian are essential to an understanding of the
period with which Cochrane's great book deals, and they furnish
indeed the vantage point from which he attacks the subject.

In the work of Cochrane the teaching of Milner and of Hutton
achieved one of its permanent results. They had much to do
with producing the man who produced the books; and since it
was a man that they helped to produce, he differed from both
of them in emphasis and inference: he made his own analysis
and reached his own conclusions. To him Thucydides, rather
than Aristotle, seemed to exemplify the Greek mind, not at its
most characteristic, but at its best; and for that best he developed
and always retained a profound sympathy. But Hutton's sense
of the contrast and tension between much in the classical outlook
and the Christian seems also to have borne its fruit. *Christianity
and Classical Culture* is a study in contrast, but pursued with a
completeness and balance for which Hutton never cared to
labour and with a sense of the importance of first principles that
is more reminiscent of Milner. And the contrast, after all, is not
unrelieved: the realism of Thucydides finds its completion in
St. Augustine. . . . Cochrane's achievement was admirably described by Innis: "it represents the flowering of a long tradition
of classical scholarship in University College and at Oxford.
His roots were in Ontario soil. His robust independence of word
and phrase reflected his background. His concern not only with

the role of thought in Graeco-Roman civilization, but with its reflection in the work of the great historians of that civilization, enabled him to make the first major Canadian contribution to the intellectual history of the West."

So far the chief external influence noticed, whether as operating directly or indirectly, has been Oxford "Greats." With the advent of Gilbert Norwood, a fresh influence, this time from Cambridge, came into play. It was more distinctively literary, certainly not at all ethical or political, in reference, and much less addicted to philosophical generalization. In support of the new influence Norwood brought the prestige of a name already distinguished in classical studies, with *Greek Tragedy*, *The Art of Terence*, *The Greek Writers*, and numerous articles, notes, and reviews, already in print. To this list the years at University College saw important additions: *Greek Comedy*, a revised edition of *Greek Tragedy*, *Plautus and Terence* (in the series "Our Debt to Greece and Rome"), *Pindar* (the Sather Classical Lectures, University of California, 1945), *Essays on Euripidean Drama* (appropriately to be issued jointly by the Toronto, Cambridge, and California University Presses), with over forty articles, notes, and reviews on classical subjects. The list so amply attests Norwood's special interest in Graeco-Roman drama, the field in which his reputation was largely made, that if one must select a single volume to exhibit his point of view and method, it may safely be the *Pindar*, perhaps his finest work of scholarship and criticism.

The double description is significant. The *Pindar* has two aspects: it is exact scholarship; it is also literary criticism. But the two are never disjoined: scholarship is there in support of criticism, and they meet in a common focus on the text of the individual poem. If the earlier tradition in University College started with the text and ended in generalization and far-ranging reference, the new influence was directed to a closer study of the text and a constant return to it. Every temptation was avoided to consider the wood at the expense of the trees. To the elucidation, not of Pindar or his age, but of the poems, are dedicated the eight lectures, with appendices, notes, and bibliography, running (at a guess) to two-thirds the length of the lectures themselves. For, like Bentley, Norwood knows all the commentators; but the notes, read in conjunction with the lectures, take the sting out of Jowett's gibe—so much may one man do to enliven otherwise indifferent company.

The exploration of Pindar's meaning proceeds at two levels. The first is linguistic: the diligent search for the exact and full meaning of the words he employs, pursued with an erudite eye on both etymology and usage. Sometimes the result is to correct translators and commentators; sometimes to confirm the commentator and, momentarily, to intensify the apparent ineptitude of which he has complained. But precisely at this point the second level on which the problem of meaning must be attacked demands attention: not the linguistic, but the poetic—that is, the words considered in the context of the whole poem. For only this context will enable the critic to determine the particular meaning which carries for the poet the requisite suggestion. Thus stated, the principle is applicable, in varying degree, to the language of any good poem and of all good poets. But it is specially applicable, and indeed indispensable, in the reading of Pindar, whose use of language is in a peculiar way "symbolic." It is as if from the poet's contemplation of the event which he is to celebrate and its attendant circumstances, from what he wishes to say and the myths which he determines to employ, there emerges a concrete image—of a rose, it may be, or a river, a measuring line or a bee—which becomes for him the symbol of this poem or of the total aesthetic experience which the poem embodies. And this concrete image, this "objective correlative" (for so, by a conscious transposition, one might describe it though our critic does not), this symbol, may govern the evolution of the ode, colour its language and imagery, and lie at the root of the meaning—almost, one might say, be its meaning. This is the theory which the *Pindar* propounds and which it applies to the elucidation and criticism of many of the odes.

Supporting, and in some degree suggesting, this theory is a view of poetry, and of criticism, grounded on an emphatic affirmation of art for art's sake. Poetry is *sui generis*. It may indeed embody a man's conceptions and beliefs in religion, ethics, politics, what you will; but the truth or falsehood, consistency or inconsistency, sense or nonsense of these, have no bearing on the power or value of the poem, which reside solely in its evocation of beauty, Norwood's statement of the position is indeed more unqualified than Pater's. Consciously or unconsciously Pindar's motive was the creation of beauty, and it is the preoccupation of commentators with his beliefs and opinions that has obscured this fact and put the theory of the symbol beyond their reach. Influenced as he no doubt was by Pater, Norwood's theory and method present analogies with later schools of criticism, as our lifting of a famous phrase from T. S. Eliot was designed to suggest. His denial of all similarity between Pindar and the modern Symbolists must be taken as a disavowal of their influence upon his own use of the concept. His insistence on the image, however, as the essence of poetry, the key to the poem's meaning and the primary concern of criticism, suggests some analogy with the New Critics, so called. But here the difference is at least as notable as the similarity, and the difference is all in Norwood's favour. His study of imagery is pursued in the context of the whole poem and with steady reference to its structure, pursued too with the support of linguistic learning as wide as it is exact, with comparisons drawn from six literatures, and (for all his concentration on the text as alone able finally to reveal its own meaning) with a clear sense of Pindar's location in history and its bearing on the character of his art, as frequent references, and three or four luminous pages in the final lecture, join to attest. One would like to recommend to the New Critics a careful perusal of Norwood on Pindar.

Norwood's emphasis on literature in the stricter meaning of the term was strongly reinforced by E. T. Owen, whose background was entirely different. A Canadian, Owen had received his initial training at Trinity College before its federation in the University; but so independent a mind would have been much the same whatever the influences brought to bear upon it. With little of Norwood's gusto, his far-ranging curiosity, or his breadth and weight of erudition, Owen had read intensively and thought long

and deeply on the subjects with which he chose to deal. He was
first and last a literary critic, whose sound scholarship was used
in the service of criticism, but to support and safeguard his critical reading of the poem rather than to guide it. Until his last
years he published little, finding in his classroom a more con-
genial medium. But out of his teaching of Homer, Aeschylus,
and Sophocles at University College, there came four or five
essays of rare distinction for the *Quarterly*; later he prepared
his lectures on the *Iliad* for publication, and he left a volume on
Aeschylus, which has appeared since his death.

All were the fruit of his study and his teaching, and they have
certain features in common: they are exclusively literary in
reference, concentrating upon the poem as a work of art and
seeking to isolate its effect and the methods by which the effect
is achieved; in this they pay primary attention not to imagery
but to action and structure; they are historical in so far as the
mode of the work's original delivery can be shown to have
carried its own conventions and to have conditioned the effect
and the devices necessary to attain it; and they altogether eschew
generalization. The book on Homer bears the curious and (at
first glance) tautological title, *The Story of the Iliad as Told in the
Iliad*, and each of the essays on Greek tragedy centres on a single
play. But this absence of generalization, this rigorous particu-
larity, do not mean that Owen entertained no clear view of the
nature of poetry and the function of criticism; quite the contrary.
Only, he insisted that the business of the critic was to elucidate
the poem, and its true effectiveness, and that, in order to do so,
he should recognize the kind of poetry it was and disregard all
other matters. Thus he refuses to concern himself with the
Homeric question, much less with the *Iliad* as embodying a
particular stage of political, ethical, or religious development.
Through whatever process it reached its present form, and whatever its implications as an historical document, it was essentially
the world's greatest example of oral story-telling in verse, whose
effects and the devices by which they were achieved bore every
appearance of conscious art and at all events could be formulated and expounded by the critic only in terms of conscious art.

Owen's exclusively literary reference did not, where occasion demanded, preclude his recognition that ethical and religious beliefs might enter deeply into the poet's intention and effects. He agrees with MacNeile Dixon, that Aeschylus was, "beyond all dramatists, a theologian, . . . turning always back from earthly scenes and events to the primal and ultimate things, the beginnings, ends and purposes of the world." His recurrent theme was the evolution of man's ethical ideals and man's effort to interpret the world, and finally the gods, in their light. This is perfectly apparent in the one surviving trilogy, the *Oresteia*: in the *Agamemnon* the act of justice is vitiated by crime and itself demands the punishment executed by Orestes, in the *Libation-Bearers*, at the command of Apollo, the voice of Zeus. Though here the motive is purely that of duty, the deed, and by implication the command from which it springs, perpetuating violence, offend the instincts of civilized man, and hence breed the remorse symbolized in the flight of Orestes pursued by the Erinyes. But this is not the end. In the *Eumenides* a new outlook and a reconciliation are achieved when Athena receives Orestes into her protection, a jury of Athenians gives verdict in his favour, and the Erinyes find a resting place in the city as the guardians of its justice. This is the pattern of Aeschylus' thought, of what Owen calls "the harmony of Aeschylus," in whose light we can interpret his other plays, and especially can interpret the *Prometheus* as a stage in the education, that is, in the evolving conception, of Zeus himself. Only Aeschylus' medium was poetry, not rational theology, and the result was neither argument nor dogma, but vision. His ethical and theological purpose was not extraneous, but of the essence of his poetry; and the choric drama, the particular form in which he recast and reinterpreted the ancient legends which had embodied primitive conceptions, was peculiarly suited to his purpose, since this drama was itself religious ritual with power to effect what it presented. This is the frame of reference in which Aeschylus' tragedy should be treated if his full power is to be recognized, instead of being viewed as a first movement towards realistic drama, with which in fact it has little in common.

The Story of the Iliad and *The Harmony of Aeschylus* deserve, in their very different field, a reputation as high and as wide as Cochrane's; for they reveal Owen as a literary critic unsurpassed in sensitivity, penetration, and independence of judgment. If they become more widely known, they can hardly fail of this reputation; if they do not, the qualities which they manifest have done their full service in the classroom, the medium of Owen's own choice.

The range of classical studies in University College has been impressive. One major field was indeed omitted, classical archaeology, but the defect was very largely made good by the Royal Ontario Museum, with, in recent years, the brilliant work of Dr. Homer Thompson.

Not the ancient classical world alone, but also ancient Israel, with the peoples surrounding it, became the object of a sustained and carefully organized educational effort and, in University College, of intense scholarly activity and finally of distinguished publication; and here the interest in archaeology was present from the first.

The leading spirit in the first generation was J. F. McCurdy, whose massive *History, Prophecy and the Monuments* established his reputation as a scholar and gave a clear indication of much that was, and was to be, characteristic of the Department. In the Preface, he explains the interest and importance of the history and literature of the Hebrew people, adequately considered, and, in view of their vast contribution to the religious thought of the West, their claim to a place in any scheme of liberal education. By *adequately considered*, he means studied with a due sense of their sacred character, but without prejudice and with all the resources of scholarship freely brought to bear upon the subject, and above all with a thorough application of historical method. In *History, Prophecy and the Monuments*, even the layman can appreciate the comprehensiveness of the investigation, the presence of a detailed knowledge, linguistic, archaeological, and literary, the consistent effort to interpret the facts brought to light, and the attempt to serve thereby at once the student and the intelligent general reader. The manner strikes one as old-fashioned and the style as somewhat rotund, but in its learning and its principles of interpretation the work was in the vanguard in its day and its argument is never obscure. To McCurdy are owing not only the foundations of the honour course in his subject, not only the tradition of scholarship in the Department which has given it a high place in graduate studies and research, but also its multiple interest in linguistic, archaeological, historical, and literary investigation, and in biblical criticism and liberal theology, all of which were continued and developed under W. R. Taylor.

Taylor was McCurdy's student, and chosen substitute and successor, who shared his outlook and the majority of his interests and aims. Three in particular are easy to recognize: the interest in Hebrew history, interpreted by the best standards of historical scholarship and in the light of its relation to the whole history of the Near and Middle East; the literary study of the Old Testament, in which Taylor's superior gifts as a literary critic gave him a marked advantage; and the concern with the modern developments of biblical scholarship and liberal theology, in which Taylor's natural bent for philosophical inquiry and generalization again gave him an advantage. Much of his time and effort went to the work of his Department and to his own teaching. Under him the Department expanded and increased in prestige. In his view teaching always came first. He was an admirable expositor and critic, and besides his honour courses, pass "Oriental Literature," the equivalent in University College for "Religious Knowledge," came to discharge an important function in the educational scheme. His literary taste and skill received their lasting monument shortly after his death in his translation of the Psalms in the New American Revised Version, on whose board he had represented Canada and on which he bestowed years of loving labour. He also left ready for publication a Commentary on the Psalms, and his interest in philosophical theology issued in valuable papers in the *Quarterly* and other journals.

During Taylor's administration of the Department, it gained immensely in international reputation through the very extensive and distinguished scholarly output of T. J. Meek. A noted authority on the Hebrew language, with numerous original contributions to his credit, and a principal translator of *The Bible: An American Translation,* and its joint editor, Meek also did important work in archaeology, in the course of which he developed a special interest in ancient law. The result is seen in his later work, in his volume of *Old Akkadian Texts* and in his translations in *Ancient Near Eastern Texts* (ed. Pritchard). Though concerned mainly with research in the stricter sense, Meek has always had in view the bearing of research on interpretation. Nor has he been unmindful of the claims of the student and the general reader. His most important work in this kind is his *Hebrew Origins.* Originally written as the Haskell Lectures at Oberlin for 1933-34, the book was largely rewritten for its revised edition (1950). In the Preface of the first edition Meek says: "The material, as conditioned by its presentation to a lay audience, is semipopular in character, but at the same time it is sufficiently technical and original, I trust, to interest the specialist as well. . . . The book is fully documented with references, as I feel all books should be." No volume could give a more adequate conspectus of Meek's interests and his range of learning, linguistic, archaeological, and in the fields of primitive law and comparative religion, as it deals with the origin of the Hebrew people itself, Hebrew law, the Hebrew God, the priesthood, prophecy, and (finally) monotheism. To place *Hebrew Origins* beside *History, Prophecy and the Monuments* is to realize the strides which studies in this field have taken in the past half-century and something of the contribution which members of University College have made to them.

In the apportioning of subjects between the University and the Colleges, the Classics and Orientals at least suffered no violence; but Philosophy was arbitrarily divided, with Ethics assigned to the Colleges and all the rest to the University. This perhaps accounts for the fact that the holders of the chair of Ethics in University College have won their laurels in other fields. Frederick Tracy, whose scholarly and finished lectures in

Ethics made a lasting impression on his students, owed his reputation outside the College to pioneer work in child psychology, with his *Psychology of Childhood*, which went through numerous editions and was translated into various foreign languages. His successor, G. S. Brett, who held the chair in conjunction with that of Philosophy in the University, was essentially an historian of thought and produced only one study which could be classed as Ethics, his *Government of Man*. Nevertheless, a strong ethical interest is apparent in the work of both Tracy and Brett.

Brett's great *History of Psychology* immediately became, as its successive volumes appeared, and has ever since remained, the standard work in English on the subject. After forty years, I am credibly informed, the famous first volume requires hardly any revision for the new edition now being prepared. This volume, which deals with the classical and patristic periods, and with ancient Hebrew and Indian literature, entails the delicate task of separating the as yet undifferentiated subject of psychology from the general philosophy of nature and man or from matters specifically theological, while at the same time preserving a sense of its setting in these contexts; and this task Brett performs to admiration, being indeed specially equipped by his interests and his abilities therefor. Perhaps the readiest way to get some first-hand knowledge of these interests and abilities is to read *Psychology Ancient and Modern*, his contribution to the series "Our Debt to Greece and Rome," since there are summed up many of the conclusions reached in his long *History of Psychology*. Three brief quotations from this volume will at least illustrate its suggestiveness. The great merit of Plato and Aristotle, he explains, and the source of their later influence, lay not in their solutions, but in their formulation of problems and their discovery of method:

It is a matter of perpetual wonder that the Greek thinkers could develop a problem and a method at a time when the available data made correct solutions impossible. To suggest the right problem and view it from the right point of view is a mark of genius and also the greatest contribution that one person or century can bequeath to subsequent generations.

The tradition that Plato taught a doctrine of innate ideas and that [modern] empiricism delivered mankind from this incubus, is a curious aberration of the historians. But there was some ground for it and it is worth while to rehearse the evidence. . . .

In declaring thought impossible without imagination Aristotle subscribes to a theory which is truly empirical, but not limited to sensationalism. Since the reason is really the "place of forms," and the act of reasoning is selection and rejection of images, the reason must itself be an immanent power. . . . Many psychologists seem to forget that a science deals with the parts of a whole and therefore always assumes but never needs to discuss the whole itself. There is no science of the Universe, but all sciences presuppose the Universe. If psychology is not a science of the soul but only of phenomena, that is true mainly because it presupposes the soul as the basis of the phenomena.

And, one may add, nothing in the book is better, or more characteristic of its author, than the luminous pages of the concluding chapter, too long to quote, on the influence of Aristotle upon Machiavelli, Melanchthon, and Hobbes.

With *The Government of Man,* and his numerous papers, which range from technical discussions of Aristotle on tragedy or Newton and religious thought to popular expositions of Santayana or Schweitzer, these volumes on the history of psychology illustrate the qualities which made Brett so effective and stimulating an expositor whether in the spoken or the written word. His teaching had as it were two pivotal points: the critical examination of original texts grounded on a thorough knowledge of the language in which they were written, and his sense of historical setting and development. "Without some knowledge of its setting," he remarks, "the text is read in vain." Old students agree that Brett's most distinctive qualities were his power of penetrating through the obsolete formulation of a question or attempted solution to its full meaning and recognizing therein its kinship with later investigations, and his power of summing up the essence of an outlook, a method, or an individual thinker. Undoubtedly Brett's work reflected the natural bent of his mind, but also that bent as it was fostered at Oxford; for with Brett we return to the influence of "Greats" on the scholarship and teaching of University College. From the basic training in *Literae Humaniores* might emerge, as interest was fired and later study confirmed it, a classicist, an historian, or a philosopher, but whichever direction subsequent specialization took, the other two influences would make their presence felt. So for Brett "Greats" proved an entrance to the whole history of philosophy, ancient and modern, and to a special interest in scientific method and the relations of science and philosophy; but the primacy of the great Greek thinkers, and especially Aristotle, was never forgotten, and the importance of the text and the language in which it was written balanced the sense of historical development and the encyclopaedic learning which he acquired. In this (as he would readily have affirmed) the example and influence of his tutor, J. L. Myres, were formative.

The twofold emphasis on texts and historical development left its mark not only on Brett's writing and teaching, but on his reorganization of the honour course in Philosophy, and the shaping of his special favourite, Philosophy with English or History. He was eager to meet the needs of other departments for appropriate courses in his subject, and under his leadership Philosophy achieved a position of influence in the University almost without contemporary parallel in any other institution.

In the modern European languages we have glanced at the work of Squair, de Champ, and Needler, with a promise to return briefly to the first-named. Fraser and Squair's *French Grammar* was a book of first-rate importance and influence in its day and kind. It left a deep impress on the teaching of the language in Ontario and extended its sway far beyond the Province, to the rest of Canada, the United States, and Great Britain. While the full and systematic study of grammar as the necessary foundation for genuine competence in the reading, writing, and speaking of French gives us the centre of Squair's interest and influence, it does not exhaust them. Conscious of the values which only a Frenchman could exemplify and impart, he brought in de Champ, who became for generations of students in University College an institution. Nor was this all. In his autobiography Squair illustrates the kind of examination questions asked in the history of French literature before his day—questions about books and even authors that the student had not read, and tells us how he vowed, if the power were ever given him, to reform this "crying evil." He kept his promise: he insisted on the careful reading of a generous body of representative texts arranged on an historical plan, and as background therefor he provided studies in French political and social history and in the art and architecture of France. Without himself being a profound scholar or an original critic in these fields, he not only shaped a sound set of honour courses, but supplied a framework in which the more impressive scholarly and critical contributions of J. S. Will and (until his translation to the chair of French at Cambridge) F. C. Green could find a place. Will, who published relatively little, did his best work with his advanced students at the honour and graduate levels, as many of them have testified. Green was writing steadily during his years at Toronto. Without troubling to formulate any distinctive theory of the nature of literature or the function of the critic, he presented with gusto, and a degree of genial cynicism, the results of wide reading in French literature and its social background. His two books on the history of the French novel offer an informative and stimulating introduction to the subject, which won the praise of many —among others, of Arnold Bennett. Later he was to present more detailed studies of two novelists, Stendhal and Proust. But his interests extended beyond fiction to drama, and into the field of comparative literature. *Minuet*, his comparison of French and English literature in the eighteenth century, is written with his usual vigour and suggestiveness, though some of its rapid generalizations might give a more cautious spirit pause. With these names may be mentioned that of Allen, who added to his work in Romance philology a comparative study of the languages of the North American Indian, unfortunately cut short by his early death.

For anyone who graduated in the first thirty-five years of our period, English and Alexander became almost interchangeable terms. The least domineering of men, he dominated the scene by the power of his mind and personality, and he left a mark upon the teaching of English in the University, and in the schools, which continues to this day—and long may it continue!

With his friend G. M. Wrong he shaped the honour course in English and History. Trained in Classics himself (Gildersleeve regarded him as the most gifted of his students on the literary side), he set a special value on English and History with the Classical option. Times have changed and the long and distinguished partnership known as "English and History" has been terminated; but English Language and Literature, its successor, has been careful to keep open the possibility of combining English with History, with Classical or Modern Languages, and also, in reflection of another of Alexander's prime interests, with Philosophy.

Underlying Alexander's whole effort was a very definite conception of literature and its role in liberal education (and here again I may perhaps be allowed to draw on a more extended account which I wrote, for the *University of Toronto Quarterly*, at the time of his death). In its widest definition, he observes, "literature is written thought. . . . This is our material, be the nature of the ideas or the form of the expression what they may." It includes *The Origin of Species* as well as the *Iliad* and *Lear*, whatever indeed is addressed to the general reader; and as addressed to the general reader it is or may be considered by the student of letters. Literature in a stricter sense is required to present its thought "powerfully, appropriately and beautifully" or to possess "style" with its expression of a personality and its colouring of emotion. But by literature in a yet stricter sense we mean imaginative literature wherein the writer does not merely shape and colour his material but creates it and, to present truth as he sees it, resorts to fiction. And, finally, when this imaginative content "is expressed with the highest beauty, fitness and power, it receives an additional element of form and becomes poetry." Form and thought may be isolated as subjects of critical attention, "but they cannot in reality be separated. . . . The more perfect and the higher is the poetry, the more inseparably and organically are thought and form interwoven." In all its higher reaches, and particularly in poetry, literature has for its end, or at least its accompaniment, pleasure. As a means of education—and it is in this context that he most commonly speaks of it—literature has knowledge of the highest value to bestow, not in the main a knowledge of particular subjects, but of life and human nature as they are presented by minds more than commonly percipient and acute. Reading is vicarious experience. But in order that it may discharge this office, the experience must be entered into, lived through; and this can happen only as the reader's interest is quickened and he comes to read the book for its own sake, for the pleasure of the process. Wide reading makes you free of the best society in the world; but as social intercourse will yield its benefits only as it is enjoyed, so with the society of books. Among the benefits accruing from the study of literature none is greater than the entry which it gives into the realm of art by awakening the perception of formal beauty; but formal beauty, again, can be perceived only as it is enjoyed. Thus the principle that the end of poetry, of imaginative literature, is pleasure is as securely built into Alexander's definition as is that other Aristotelian principle, that poetry is an imitation of nature, whose substance is truth if its vehicle is fiction.

In his pyramid of definitions, each more exacting than its predecessor, every step is significant: the wide range of the primary definition (literature included, and a department of literature must concern itself, he insisted, with much besides *belles-lettres*); the wholesome emphasis on intellectual content; the clear recognition, however, that thought in literature is addressed to the general reader and must be treated by the critic with a constant sense of this fact, that the thought exists and is operative in closest organic relation with other elements, and that the work as a work of art is the embodiment of a unified and unifying experience dependent upon the total sensibility of the poet. This last fact he sought to record by his emphasis upon subjectivity and emotion, terms acceptable in his earlier days, but not perhaps the most fortunate, as he himself came to feel.

In his Inaugural at University College, most of these ideas are set forth, and the rest in subsequent essays: "The Study of Literature," "Poetry: Its Thought and Form," "The Nature and

Office of Poetry." Together they give us the basis of his work as teacher and educator, and a clear indication of the aims and methods of English at Toronto, from the concentration on individual works, the primary necessity, through the comprehension, in terms at once historical and critical, of the principal periods, to some sense of the whole majestic sweep of English literature from its earliest beginnings "to its culmination in the multifarious streams of literary activity amid which we ourselves live."

Of Alexander's treatment of individual authors (Shakespeare, Wordsworth and Coleridge, Keats, Carlyle and Arnold, above all, Shelley and Browning) there is no space to speak. Much of it was communicated only in his lectures, in which analyses of particular works, as lucid as they were sensitive, played an important part; some found its way into a long succession of *Select Poems*, or into his edition of Shelley, his *Introduction to Browning*, or half-a-dozen articles in various journals. Of it all, printed and unprinted, one may safely say that it was the equal of, and on Shelley and Browning superior to, the best academic criticism in his period. This was my impression as an undergraduate, and a careful re-reading of everything that he published has served only to confirm it.

As time went on, Alexander gathered around him able colleagues: first, Malcolm Wallace, then Clawson, erudite and meticulous, then George Stevenson, whose early death cut short a career as teacher and scholar rich in achievement and richer in promise, and finally Herbert Davis, whom one imagines strolling through the Cloisters in the '20's, with the *London Mercury* under his arm and followed by the admiring gaze of undergraduates, the destiny as yet hidden which was to make him one of the foremost authorities on Swift and carry him, after his tenure of the chair at Cornell and the presidency of Smith College, to the readership in Textual Criticism at Oxford.

Once, on a public occasion which many will recall, Alexander said, "I count this my greatest service to University College: I appointed Malcolm Wallace to the staff." His student, his devoted friend and colleague, and his successor, Wallace carried on the Alexander tradition in English. Yet they were sufficiently unlike to be complementary. As a teacher his method and manner differed from Alexander's. Wallace could draw out the most diffident of students, while Alexander (in spite of himself) awed the most self-confident. It was not a question of manner alone. More than Alexander's, Wallace's interests were strongly ethical and, in a large sense, political in their colouring: Milton, for example, was an author to be placed in his historical setting, but (this duly accomplished) he was a man whose ideas must be brought to the test of our own time and judged by their wisdom and utility, and this was a matter on which any intelligent undergraduate, under Wallace's encouragement, might hazard an opinion. No one who has read the admirable essay on Milton in Wallace's edition of the *Selected Prose*, or his Alexander Lectures on the spirit which animates English literature, will fail to appreciate the interest and stimulus to be afforded by this way of looking at his subjects, or at the same time its divergence from Alexander's more purely literary and philosophical approach. The interest in the human and the ethical, placed in their historical setting, also led Wallace to biography and to his most important piece of research. In the preface to his *Life of Sir Philip Sidney* he quotes with approval Meredith's words: "We cannot come to a right judgment in biography unless we are grounded in history"; and again: "Real greatness must be based on morality." These two principles underlie a narrative of Sidney's life and times, which is an important contribution to knowledge, and a judgment of his character, whose insight and authority have never been questioned.

Almost the last student to come under Alexander's personal influence as a teacher, and the last of our notables, was E. K. Brown, who joined the staff after Alexander's retirement. It is doubtful whether any member of the College ever made a greater impression upon his students than did Brown, whose effectiveness at all levels was astonishing. His superb native endowment had been assiduously cultivated at every opportunity, and the first great opportunity, the fundamental influence, had been the teaching and the example of Alexander. The years at University College, before his brief sojourn at Cornell in succession to Davis and his final post at Chicago, were years of preparation for his mature work in scholarship and criticism; but his interest had already turned to Canadian poetry, with his annual surveys in the *Quarterly*, and he was busy on Matthew Arnold, on the art of the novel, and on American fiction, the subject-matter of the four books which he lived to write after leaving Toronto and before his tragically early death. One of these, *Rhythm in the Novel*, his Alexander Lectures, contains a tribute to his first teacher which leaves us in no doubt of the profound and lasting influence upon him: he had heard every one of Alexander's lecture courses at least twice.

And so we come back to Alexander once more, and his power as a teacher. Much has been said in this essay of the honour courses, and properly, for they are the proudest achievement of the Faculty of Arts and one in which University College played a decisive role. But Alexander's power was felt by honour-men and pass-men alike. One will not soon forget the hushed attention of the mixed audience that crowded the lecture theatre to hear him expound Browning or read Rossetti's "Sister Helen." It is not easy to explain the secret of that amazing success. He was not a spectacular lecturer: he disdained the tricks of the trade, and emotionalism withered in his presence. But the combination of critical ability of a very high order, a unique capacity for cogent exposition, and skill in interpretative reading, free from every hint of the elocutionist's art, proved irresistible. His emphasis was always on the essential meaning, embracing intellectual content, feeling, and art, which in the poem became one and indivisible, the outcome of a unifying experience. In most cases he led us to that full meaning, that unifying experience, by first expounding the poem's content, its meaning in the more restricted sense, thus securing a firm foundation for whatever he had to say of feeling and of artistry. Often it was not necessary to say very much: the feeling and the artistry were borne in upon us in the very terms of the exposition and in the reading that accompanied it. So he brought us, almost unawares, to the experience which was the full meaning of the poem. And if this be not the best way to teach poetry, who shall show us a better?

The main significance of the notables in the history of University College since Federation emerges with a fair degree of clarity. The first generation (e.g., Hutton, Milner, McCurdy, Alexander) established the strong tradition of scholarly, illuminating, and stimulating teaching as the first duty of the Staff, at the very time when undergraduate teaching began in many North American institutions to be subordinated and sacrificed to research. In establishing this tradition they were aided by the existence of the idea of the honour course: a course which both in the nature of its subject-matter and in the quality of its best students would offer a challenge to the thought and scholarship of the instructor. But before these potentialities could be fully realized, the idea of the honour course itself required to be implemented and exploited; this was in large measure the work of the first generation. Here, with Oxford "Greats" as a strong initial influence, Classics led the way. But other departments followed in applying principles held in common: the selection of an important area to furnish the principal subject-matter and the focus of a four-year course; the insistence on a critical reading of texts (and hence on the necessary basis in language) as the foundation of the whole process; the steady emphasis on historical method and on history learned from, or in close connection with, the study of texts; and, finally, as an adequate understanding was achieved, the invitation to bring to the bar of experience and judgment the content and form of the authors read.

In the second generation (and the third, of which few examples fall within the terms of this essay), two developments are evident: in the first place, as the gains made by the first generation were consolidated, new men were imported from without, some to fortify the tradition established, others to complement or modify it; and, secondly, to the effort of teaching and of shaping the educational system was gradually added a list of distinguished publications in various fields, so that the College began to take its place in the republic of letters. But between the honour teaching (with presently teaching also at the graduate level) and the publications there were strong lines of connection and mutual influence. The publications were rarely those of narrow or purely factual research, but works rather of interpretation and criticism, whose ideas, very often, had been conceived and developed in connection with honour and graduate teaching, and had served to inspire and invigorate that teaching.

Thus the achievement of the notables sprang from, and found support in, the academic life and activities of the College. Nor was their work done in isolation, but as members of a community of scholars, a continuing body, constantly depleted and as constantly replenished. Of this community the notables are in a special sense the representatives, the men who, in their generation, most fully realized and most effectively exhibited the ethos and the value of University College as an institution of higher learning.

CLAUDE T. BISSELL

Opinion

IN A LETTER that he wrote to the student editors of a University of Toronto journal commending their critical attitude towards staff and curriculum, Stephen Leacock observed that "I am even inclined, as a professor, to harbour a little bit of academic discontent of my own." He went on to argue, in a cheerfully iconoclastic vein, "that our colleges would be greatly brightened if there were no students; if the professor could saunter undisturbed among the elm trees in friendly colloquy, lecturing—for they know no other form of conversation—to one another; if the library and the campus could enjoy at all seasons the quiet hush that now only falls on them in August; if the deep peace where learning loves to brood were never broken by examinations and roll-calls. . . ." Stephen Leacock did not say what he thought the course of events would be if this professorial dream were realized. But I suspect that eventually the professors would become bored with each other and would long for the old dispensation. They would find themselves listening expectantly for the voice of the student raised in question or in protest, shaping in words an exploded platitude, a wise and realistic insight, or a grandly Utopian ideal.

The University College student has been accused at various times of a lack of dogmatic conviction, but never of inarticulateness. His most characteristic observations, those made during non-curricular seminars in residence and common room, are, unfortunately, lost to the historian. Even his observations of a more formal kind, those made during the course of debate, for

instance, are preserved only in the minutes of societies. The voice of the student raised in debate must have had a particularly compulsive ring at various times, especially during the '90's of the last century when debates in the Literary and Scientific Society were led by such men as Arthur Meighen, Mackenzie King, and G. Howard Ferguson. There is, however, one unfading source to which we can turn for an expression through the years of student ideas and attitudes—unrepresentative and unreliable although, at times, it may be. That source is student literary publications.

The record of student literary publications at University College really begins with the first issue of *The Varsity* on October 7, 1880. Before that the Literary and Scientific Society had produced one *Annual*, or report of its activities, and in the late '70's a weekly paper entitled *The White and Blue* had prepared the way for *The Varsity*. From its very first number *The Varsity* displayed a vigour and self-confidence that marked it out for survival. When in 1887 the University Federation Act was passed, *The Varsity* was one of the most durable assets to which the newly constituted University of Toronto fell heir. Up until that time, *The Varsity* had been exclusively a publication of University College, since the University of Toronto could be said to exist only as an idea that had its actuality in University College. Even after the setting up of a professoriate distinct from the staff of University College and the rapid expansion of the University, *The Varsity* remained for many years primarily the publication of University College.

The early *Varsity* was not a newspaper. It was, to use its own explanatory sub-title, "A Weekly Review of Education, University Politics, and Events." It was sold on stands or by subscriptions, and its fortunes—editorial and financial—were in the hands of shareholders who together made up The Varsity Publishing Company. University graduates took a vigorous part in its early direction; indeed it was not until the fourth year of publication that an undergraduate became editor-in-chief. Contributions from graduates—some of them long departed from the College halls—made up a fair proportion of its pages. And even the non-graduate, provided he had earned a name in journalism or in literature, was warmly received. While reaching out and appealing to a wide audience, *The Varsity* still retained its identity as a College publication. Its strongest appeal was to the College audience: to students, graduates, and staff. When in October 1883 it was officially adopted by the Executive Committee of Convocation, it became in fact what in theory it had always aspired to be— the spokesman for the College community.

There was little danger, then, that *The Varsity* would grow weak on a diet of undergraduate trivialities. If anything, the danger lay in the opposite extreme—in a tendency to regard its role with an overweening solemnity. The first editorial was a cloudy, polysyllabic proclamation of principles. In a final effort at summary the editor wrote: "In reality our intentions are very demure: not a guiding star, not an interpreter, but a register of opinion in and out of the University in matters of education; an unbiassed annalist of University life; and, in this last connexion, a strenuous advocate of what constitutes well-being." The Olympian air and ornate vocabulary alarmed some of the early readers, one of whom was moved in a letter to express the hope that "the editors have no such intention of allowing the paper to become the organ of a numerous but most objectionable class of University students—the prigs—men who are so thoroughly impressed with the dignity of the undergraduate that they quite look down on all manly exercise, who assume the habits and demeanour of the Methodist parson, and who talk as though their spare hours were spent in learning by heart the unabridged edition of Webster's dictionary. . . ." The earnestness of the editors was amusingly reflected in the title-page. In its earliest form it consisted of an elaborate group of figures and objects: the dominating figure is presumably Minerva, who is flanked on one side by a man and on the other by a woman, each wearing a complete set of academicals; behind them is a representation of University College, and in front of them, among a group of symbolical objects, is an open book upon which are inscribed the words "Amica ante omnes philosophia." After a few issues, the design was compressed and simplified, but the general effect was unchanged: Minerva is reduced to a sculptured head; the gentleman and lady are now definitely undergraduates of a pensive cast of mind; the open book remains and the motto (irreverently translated by a contemporary American college journal as "My dear, before all, I love Sophia") is given prominence.

As one might expect, *The Varsity* of these years was not an assiduous chronicler of events; frequently it built its articles and discussions on facts that may have been well known to the small, closely knit college body of the time, but that escape the modern reader. Its reporting was of a sober factual variety: résumés of the programme and the chief speeches at the meetings of the Literary and Scientific Society, and at the meetings of the other clubs and organizations that, founded recently, were exhibiting a precocious growth—the Natural Science Association, the Mathematical and Physical Society, the Modern Language Club, the Metaphysical and Political Science Club, the University Temperance League. Important speeches, such as the Convocation Address of President Daniel Wilson, the Inaugural Speech of the President of the Literary and Scientific Society, or the lecture of a visiting dignitary such as Alfred Russell Wallace were given *in extenso* without the benefit of editorial selection and exegesis.

In general, *The Varsity* as recorder of student affairs observed a self-denying ordinance. Only occasionally did it swerve from this course. To the Conversazione for 1866—the great social event of the College year, what we today would call an "At Home"—*The Varsity* despatched a representative to record his impressions. Although the resulting account has about it a tone of laboured facetiousness, it does tell us something about the atmosphere that prevailed at these events, an atmosphere that might be described as one of mannerized gaiety.

After enjoying the concert, that is, the first part—for your representative is not one of those who freezes to a seat the whole night, to the defrauding of some other person—the *Varsity* man wended his way though the Star Chamber—where he inspected the souls of the University Senators through the microscopes—to the Library. Having safely passed the Cerberus at the Gate (Punch), he gazed earnestly at the books,

"As what he ne'er might see again,"

knowing well that he would never again be admitted to the Library till another year had flown.

In the Reading-rooms he noticed some students, mostly Residence men, devouring—not books and notes—but cakes and ices!

Then he wended his way along the corridors, through which sounds of music and laughter floated and echoed back again, till even the grim corbels and gargoyles seemed to have caught the spirit of the hour, and to have joined in the revelry. Presently in the far west—in Lecture Room No. 8—various phantasmagoria flitted before his vision. Vanishing and illusory were they all—as the mathematical quantities usually obtained in this room—though they amused the onlookers much more.

He gazed in wonder at the scientific apparatus and other instruments of torture here, and completed a leisurely circuit of the building with its numerous attractions. Then the *Varsity* man's dream of happiness was abruptly brought to a close by the appearance upon the scene of a breathless *chaperone*, who took his fair companion away, leaving him disconsolate. After wandering around aimlessly for a short time, he braced himself for the closing struggle at the dressing rooms, and emerged after a tight squeeze and a hard fight, with somebody else's overcoat, hat, gloves, and overshoes. Seeing that they were of a superior quality to those in which he had sallied forth at the beginning of the evening, he was quite content, and, lighting a rare Havana, he strolled leisurely away to the Varsity sanctum, ever and anon looking back at the College windows in which one by one the lights were being extinguished.

It is a pity that on extraordinary occasions the editors did not issue a few other reporting assignments. Matthew Arnold's visit to the University in February of 1884 constituted such an occasion, and the historian, perhaps not so much of English literature as of the Canadian scene, would give much for a detailed account. The editors of *The Varsity* were not unaware of the importance of the event: Matthew Arnold was one of the best known and most admired Englishmen; he was arriving in Toronto after a lecture tour in the United States which had aroused almost as much heated journalistic comment as the election tour of an American presidential candidate; and he was coming to Toronto as a guest of an old friend, Goldwin Smith, who was an acknowledged spokesman of the cause of higher education in Canada and a particularly warm friend of University College. It was hoped, indeed, that the great poet and critic would lecture under the auspices of the Literary and Scientific Society, but the arrangements could not be made, and the lectures—two hardy veterans of the American tour, "Science and Literature" and

"Numbers"—were given in Shaftesbury Hall to (as *The Varsity* reported) "large and intellectual audiences." Arnold did, however, pay at least two visits to the College, and *The Varsity* noted each of them. When at the end of the Conversazione for that year the President of the Literary and Scientific Society, Professor Ramsay Wright, referred to the future of the scheme for public lectures in Convocation Hall, he "brought to his feet Mr. Matthew Arnold, one of the hoped-for lecturers, to answer for himself as a party to the non-fulfilment of the scheme." Arnold responded with a "few charming sentences of regret." Arnold's second visit was during the day when he was accompanied by his wife and by Mr. and Mrs. Goldwin Smith. After a tour of the College, the party attended a lecture by George Paxton Young whose eloquence was famous in the community and who in a later issue of *The Varsity* was thus apostrophized:

> Thy white-haired age, revered and loved by youth,
> Thy voice the voice of Wisdom and of Truth!

It was a happy coincidence that on this occasion the lecture was on Herbert Spencer, since, as *The Varsity* knowingly observed, "Professor Young's and Matthew Arnold's opinion of Spencer lie in about the same groove." Only one Arnoldian observation during the visit was preserved: he pronounced "the University building to be one of the finest he had ever seen." Here surely speaks the apostle of sweetness if, less certainly, of light!

The *Varsity* editors had, I fear, no eye for a "story," no skill in persuading their readers that they ought to be interested in certain events and indifferent to others. What they did have in plenty was righteous indignation, and the descriptions we have of student life are often by-products of controversy. Even such a stirring event as the departure in April 1885 of the University volunteers—"K" Company of the Queen's Own Rifles—for the Northwest Rebellion might have been compressed into a Spartan report, had it not been for an attack on the conduct of the students made in the columns of *The Globe*. This, declared *The Varsity*, was "the most malicious libel yet of the many *The Globe* has published concerning the students of Toronto." In support of this statement, *The Varsity* gave a long and flattering account of the behaviour of the undergraduates: how they had assembled in front of the College and then had proceeded by a circuitous route to the station in order to avoid any possible brush with the public; how they had marched along Front Street "singing with vim 'We'll hang Louis Riel on a sour apple tree,' 'The "K's" are the boys to make the rebels fly' and other suitable adaptations"; and how they had tempered patriotic enthusiasm with courtesy, "in every instance giving way to the public and exercising the utmost self-control."

The accounts of Residence life we owe also to the *Varsity's* eagerness to embrace a cause. From random comments it is clear that the Residence men—referred to with genial irony as "the forty immortals"—were the single most influential group in the College, and that, either in themselves or through their influence on others, they generated much of the intellectual vitality that distinguished the student life of the time. And yet the Residence was an unending source of student complaints: the living quarters, especially by comparison with those available to students at the new McMaster Hall, were wretched; the steward in charge of the Residence and the dining-hall was devoted to the prospect of high profits and not to the welfare of the students—these are but a few of the complaints. *The Varsity* raised its voice more in sorrow than in anger:

If any one wishes to be convinced what a hold living in Residence has upon the average undergraduate's affections, let him survey our Residence, and then he will feel certain that no ordinary charm will persuade a man to bear with the discomfort and general slovenliness of such a place. The tie of affection must be indeed strong that will bind a man to it as his temporary home. Rooms in which there is a separate and special draft for every point of the compass—in which on a cold night the heat that a small grate fire can put forth only makes the dreary coldness of the place more apparent—rooms where the joyous sound of the broom or duster is scarcely ever heard, and where the hapless occupant can, like the mythological hero, gain new strength from close and daily contact with Mother Earth—these are some of the discomforts the inhabitants of Residence contend with. And then the meals and the appurtenances thereto—the household crockery—the spoons not free altogether from the suspicion of verdigris—the knives and forks—and last of all the tablecloth! How our memory loves to linger on the tablecloth! This article was purchased when the College was first founded, and graduates of that day have told us recently—confidentially of course—that private marks made upon it at that time were, on a recent investigation, found there still, showing that during all the intervening years it had scorned the enticements of the washerwomen. There are rooms in Residence in which the sun never shines, and the damp, unwholesome atmosphere of these is enough to beget ague. The attendance is so bad that if a man wants his room really cleaned he cleans it himself—and yet the occupants cling to the place and love it and would not leave it for the world. Can there be any stronger testimony to the value of a large Residence? Once let there be a Residence bright and attractive, with good attendance and meals, and it will be found that more even than in the past, the sons of the University will rally round the Alma Mater they have learned to love through the endearing associations of the Residence.

It will be remembered that *The Varsity* began as a "Review of Education, University Politics, and Events." The order indicates the proportionate emphasis given to each of the three areas. If "Events" were more often than not reduced to unadorned facts, "Education" and "University Politics" were attacked with expansive enthusiasm. Indeed, there is some reason for thinking that for the first few years of the decade *The Varsity* was the organ of a group of graduates who were deeply dissatisfied with the attitude of the provincial Government towards the University and with the direction given to University affairs by the official governing body, the Senate.

The Varsity was accurate in proclaiming that its interest lay in "Education" and "University Politics." It rigidly eschewed politics in the wider sense, except in so far as they bore upon educational issues. It interfered in matters of general public concern only when there was a principle involved that bore upon the conduct of higher education. Thus when in 1881 the Collector of Customs at Toronto seized the works of Paine and Voltaire, and two years later the corresponding official at Montreal added to the index the works of Huxley, Tyndall, and Spencer, *The Varsity* restated calmly and clearly the classic arguments against censorship. *The Varsity* also found itself drawn inevitably into the central dispute of the age—the relation between religion and science. Only once, however, did this question crowd others into the background. During the academic year 1885-86, Mr. A. Stevenson, a graduate of '84 and a prize essayist who was one of the *Varsity's* ablest writers, contributed

an article entitled "The New Protestantism" in which he attacked
the dogmatism of the clergy and questioned the possibility of a
free approach to theological questions in sectarian colleges. The
article elicited a series of letters, ranging in tone from sweet
reasonableness to sputtering indignation. The important point
about the affair is that all sides to what must have been (and
still is) a delicate question were given the right to state their
case, and that, editorially, *The Varsity* preserved throughout an
attitude of imperturbable calm.

On one educational issue *The Varsity* found itself involved in
an argument that reached far beyond the College walls. The
leading article in its first issue was entitled "Coeducation in
University College," and for four years—until in the spring of
1884, government legislation admitting women to the provincial
university put an end to the controversy—no topic demanded
more space and inspired more devious arguments. There were
three parties in the disputes: the die-hards, numbering among
their supporters that incredible liberal, Goldwin Smith, who
believed that women should be given an education especially
adapted to their exquisite, but minor talents, and that to admit
women to the college classroom was to plant the tree of good
and evil in an innocent paradise; the progressives, who welcomed
co-education and who pointed proudly to such universities as
Cornell and Oberlin where it had already been vindicated;
finally, the gradualists who said that women were entitled to
higher education but that they should be given separate colleges
on the model of Oxford and Cambridge. President Wilson
belonged to this last party, and, on occasion, he could find strong
support in *The Varsity*. Shortly before the admission of women
to University College, *The Varsity* fired a final protesting salvo
against co-education, arguing that "College feeling can grow up
in freedom and perfection only among men alone, and could not
be participated in or understood by women." With the first
appearance of women undergraduates in the fall of 1884, the
editors and contributors to *The Varsity* bowed gracefully to the
inevitable and turned to more fruitful topics. No sooner had the
women gained their victory than *The Varsity*, as if determined

to extract a final irony from the situation, abandoned its co-educational title-page; the three figures—the gentleman, the lady, and Minerva—disappeared, and in their place remained only the College building and the coat of arms.

The question of "hazing" was likewise an issue that aroused more than College concern. The era of organized sport was far off; and in the European tradition, student exuberance found its outlet in the normal academic life. Even Convocation was not exempt. *The Varsity* was heartily in favour of the spontaneous singing on such occasions of favourite songs, such as "Old Grimes" and "Litoria," but it frowned magisterially on "howling, horn-blowing, and cat calling." More serious was the hazing of freshmen, which often meant humiliation and physical torture to the individual. Unfortunately hazing was not, like co-education, an issue that could be settled by legislation. It was, indeed, throughout these years the great basic theme of the correspondence column; the letters played rhetorical variations on "a strong College spirit," "the virtue of manliness," or, in the opposite vein, on "affront to personal dignity" and "barbarism." A letter from H. J. Cody, a frequent speaker at the meetings of the Literary and Scientific Society, and perhaps the most brilliant student that the College had ever known, summarized the arguments of the anti-hazing party, and suggested an ingenious if Utopian method for eliminating the practice:

How, finally, can this evil thing be put away from among us? I think it can be done through the instrumentality of first year men themselves. Gentlemen of the first year, when freshmen, you are, without exception, opposed to hazing. Be consistent in your profession; continue your opposition even when you have attained to the dignity of sophomores. If you are true to yourselves and your best interests, if you remain firm in your earliest conviction throughout your college course, the "consummation devoutly to be wished" will be effected, and hazing, this "relic of barbarism," as our grand "old man eloquent" phrases it, will soon be only a subject of archaeological investigation, and lexicographers of the future will have to ransack dusty newspapers of the past to determine its meaning.

In the *Varsity*'s austere scale of journalistic values, co-education and hazing were "sensational" topics. They lay on the periphery of the two areas with which the paper was vitally concerned: what we might designate "University Politics" (to use the *Varsity's* own phrase) and "Problems of Curriculum and Methods of Education." In these two fields *The Varsity* spoke with an authority grounded on knowledge and understanding; it constitutes, I should think, a primary document for anyone interested in the development of higher education in the latter part of the nineteenth century.

In the area of "University Politics" lay questions of the internal government of the University and of its relation to the Government of the Province and to other institutions of higher learning. During the '80's *The Varsity* was, as I have pointed out, a graduate as well as an undergraduate publication, and became for a period the official spokesman of Convocation. Convocation, the assembly of all the graduates, was still a compact and manageable body; it met regularly, and spoke with an emphatic voice on College and University matters. The principal grievance was the inadequate representation of graduates on the Senate, which, as the final governing body, was the natural absorbent of popular dissatisfaction. But a more substantial grievance, this one directed against no one governing body but against Canadian society in general, was the failure to give the University strong financial support. This, said *The Varsity*, was the result of purblind government economy, and, to a lesser extent, of the immobility of Canadian wealth. It was also bound up with the constant questioning by the sectarian colleges of Toronto's title to be the Provincial (or as *The Varsity* liked to say) the National University. The main armies in the battles of the '40's and '50's between the principles of secularized and sectarian education had left the field, but intransigent guerilla bands remained to keep up the fight. The righteous curse that John Strachan had pronounced on his erring child had not been forgotten; on several occasions *The Varsity* found it necessary to protest with vehemence against the vapidly malicious attacks of the High Church *Dominion Churchman* against "the godless college."

The *Varsity's* aggressive interest in the curriculum would strike the modern student as a strange aberration, and the modern member of staff as an unexpected but refreshing demonstration of the exercise of student rights. Of course, a good deal of the comment on the curriculum, particularly detailed analysis of prescriptions, came from senior graduates, many of them actively engaged in education or even serving as University examiners. But the main "agitations" were obviously initiated by undergraduates. The demand for a professor of political economy —not to be satisfied until the appointment of Professor Ashley in 1888—and for increased emphasis within the existing curriculum on Canadian history and constitutional development, was a reflection of a growing political consciousness among the student body. Often the suggestions were the product of that radical but healthy critical spirit that will always be a mark of good college journalism. "Examinations," went a common refrain, "are barriers to the true intellectual life and should be abolished"; and (from an even more intoxicating peak of educational radicalism) "prizes and scholarships place a premium on mere diligence and powers of memory and should likewise be abolished." But, in other matters, *The Varsity* demonstrated a wise prescience, and anticipated by eighty years the deeply considered conclusions of faculty councils. In an early discussion of the relative merits of honour and pass work, *The Varsity* wrote:

What we want is not a Pass course, intended as a sort of back stairway to a degree, along which those may go who have not the requisite ability or industry to take Honours; but a general course in which there will be as much work as there is in any Honour Department, which will have as high a percentage necessary for promotion or graduation, in which there will be scholarships given, if they continue to be offered in other Honour courses, and in which a man may acquire such an education as will best fit him for succeeding in professional work and enjoying literary leisure.

In emphasizing controversy and political discussion, *The Varsity* was following in the path cleared by other contemporary periodicals, and was reflecting the legalistic and rhetorical tastes stimulated by Confederation and its aftermath. But *The Varsity*, again like its contemporaries, was aware of the refining qualities of literature—of critical discussion and assessment of writers, of descriptive and reflective essays, and, most of all, of poetry. One can discern, in the decade of the '80's, a pattern of development in which "Literature" finally assumed the dominant strand. At first, the Muse was summoned in peremptory and self-conscious tones. "Shall our Muse be silent?" the editors asked in the first issue for the year 1882.

Have we no limpid skies, sombre forests, gloomy dells, sparkling streams, beautiful faces, bright eyes to move our poetic imagination? Shall none of these have a place in our columns? Yes! the "Poets' Corner" is the most hallowed spot of that ancient shrine of the English race consecrated to the valor, the genius and the might of England. Shall we not follow so glorious an example? If we move any of our more impressionable readers to the task of committing their soul's emotion to blank or other verse, they may be sure of a kindly reception, to be followed by a niche in our Poets' Corner, a niche we hereby duly establish and consecrate.

The following Christmas *The Varsity* launched the first of its Christmas literary issues—a symposium of stories supposedly told at a Residence breakfast. And in the spring of 1885 it signalized its coming of age as a literary journal by the announcement that the directors were going to bring out in book form selections of the best prose and poetry that had appeared in *The Varsity. The Varsity Book—Prose and Poetry* appeared in the fall of 1885: a small, unpretentious volume of 200 pages, maintaining a consistent level of literary sophistication that, I suspect, no other consecutive five years of *The Varsity* could yield.

From this time to, at least, the end of the decade, *The Varsity* had no doubt of its mission. Significantly, in the first issue of 1885, the sub-title changed from "A Weekly Review of Education, University Politics, and Events" to "A Weekly Journal of Literature, University Thoughts and Events." The aim was now the "cultivating of the literary spirit" and "the establishment of a fine literary taste." The *Varsity* contributors thought of themselves not as apprentice reporters and newspaper editors, but as writers who had their place "in the drum-corps of literature,—that band of college journalists with their inexperience, their illusions, their light-hearted boyish bravery, their insufferable self-opinion, and their abundance of harmless poise, who march on the fringe of the great army, yet with a proud sense that they, too, are in the ranks." The *Varsity*'s claim to be a "Journal of Literature" was not an idle one even outside the College halls, for during these years it received contributions from almost every prominent literary figure in Canada: from established poets, such as Charles G. D. Roberts; from poets who were shortly to win critical acclaim, such as Bliss Carman and Wilfred Campbell; from popular and competent versifiers, such as Agnes Machar, Agnes Wetherald, H. K. Cockin, C. Pelham Mulvaney; from prominent *littérateurs*, such as G. Mercer Adam and T. Arnold Haultain; from historians and journalists, such as W. J. Rattray, William Houston, Henry Scadding, and J. George Hodgins.

The initial literary vigour of *The Varsity* is not a curious phenomenon, but a natural development of the time. This was the period of the Canadian renaissance in literature. Charles G. D. Roberts had ushered in the era in 1880 with his *Orion, and Other Poems*; Campbell and Lampman were to publish volumes a few years later, and Carman was just beginning to publish. This was the period, too, of the efflorescence of periodical literature: when *The Varsity* brought out its first number, *The Canadian Monthly and National Review,* conceived on the grand scale and conducted with dignity and intelligence, had still two years to run; Goldwin Smith's brilliant one-man political broadsheet, *The Bystander,* had just been launched; and three years later, *The Week,* also a Goldwin Smith brain-child, was begun and went its vigorous and authoritative way until 1896. *The Varsity* was stimulated, not overwhelmed, by this rich environment; it treated its contemporaries with respect, but not with deference; and it considered itself, with good cause, as one of the publications of the time that had a claim on the informed and intelligent reading public.

If the general cultural environment was favourable to literature, so also was the intellectual environment within the College. Although, as we have seen, *The Varsity*, no doubt echoing the convictions of many, was demanding the appointment of a professor of political economy, and, in the fervour of its cause, declared that "we would rather be able to read intelligently the works of Adam Smith, Ricardo, Malthus, J. S. Mill and Herbert Spencer than know all the extant Greek and Latin poetry by rote," the emphasis within the College was still on the study of languages, which meant primarily the study of Greek and Latin.

The study of the ancient languages was given a new impetus by
the appointment in 1880 of the popular young Oxford don,
Maurice Hutton, as Professor of Classical Literature; he gave to
the Classics course a less narrowly philological emphasis, teaching the books of the ancient world as literary masterpieces and
not as quarries for grammatical and philological lore. It was
Hutton who inspired and directed the production in April 1882
of *Antigone,* in the original Greek, referred to by *The Varsity*
some years later as one of the two or three principal events it
had sought to describe. *The Varsity* viewed with sorrow and
regret the weakening of the Classics in American universities,
but it was willing to concede that Modern languages could
provide the same kind of powerful discipline. The important
point was that university studies should train men in the art of
expression. This was the great advantage of the study of languages over the study of mathematics and natural sciences. "A
mathematician may be an acute reasoner," declared a *Varsity*
leading article, "he may be able to think out the most abstruse
problems of his science; but let him get on his feet and try to
make a speech, and what assistance is given him by his mathematical training? Great thoughts and most exact reasoning burn
within him, but alas! he cannot bring them forth, for lack of
practice in language and the art of expression." The sciences
fare no better. "They certainly teach a man to think according
to exact and systematic methods, but we confess ourselves unable
to see in what way they tend to the acquirement of power of expression." But the study of languages elicits all the desirable
qualities of mind. "By the mental labour required to master the
principles of a foreign tongue, and to discover accurately the
meaning conveyed by foreign words, the mind is trained to
think, while through the constant necessity of expressing in
English the meaning when discovered, power of expression is
acquired in the best possible way."

During the '80's the study of English language and literature
had not been placed on a sound footing. English was simply
one of the five subjects grouped under "Modern Languages,"
and, according to *The Varsity*, it consisted largely of the mem-

orization of facts about books and authors from a dull history of English literature. It was not until 1889, with the appointment of W. J. Alexander as the first full-time Professor of English, that the subject became a major discipline. But if English Literature was given only a perfunctory bow in the classroom, it was awarded a place of honour in the principal student societies. The Literary Society (the full title, "Literary and Scientific Society," was used only for impressiveness and verbal balance), was, at that time, largely what its name proclaimed. The programme of the Society consisted of the reading of essays on literary or general topics, recitations from the works of contemporary authors, and a debate, frequently on a literary topic (for example: "Resolved, that the fashionable poetry of the age—the poetry of William Morris, Rossetti, and Swinburne—is for the most part worthless"). This programme was supplemented by the Modern Language Club, where the consideration of works of literature was put on a more formal and professional basis; and by informal discussions in the Residence where the topics were of a more philosophical and metaphysical nature—these being one of the happy offshoots of residence life where the mere fact of living together in a society generates a curiosity about ultimate questions.

The Varsity was part of this literary ferment. Those who wrote for the "Lit." or the Modern Language Club were also those who wrote for *The Varsity*. In some respects, *The Varsity* was the organ of a literary cult, although never a precious and snobbish one. The beliefs of the "cult" were not narrow and dogmatic, but liberal and flexible. Still, it could take up vigorous and even combative attitudes. It welcomed the note of protest in English literature against materialism and industrialism. Carlyle, to one representative writer, was "the truest Hero and Prophet of the day"; it defended Oscar Wilde, who had been ridiculed by American papers and journals during his American tour in 1882, as essentially a co-worker with John Ruskin in the movement to bring beauty and dignity to the lives of the workers. It participated vigorously in the discussion going on in *The Week* as to whether a distinctive Canadian literature existed. On this subject, which was then, as it is now, productive of so much nonsense, it maintained a position of realistic nationalism. On the one hand, said *The Varsity*, let us get rid of servile colonialism. "Let us seek a groove in which Canadian thoughts, manners and opinions may run, and cease the vulgar endeavour to fit them to one which has been worn smooth by prejudices which have sprung from different influences and different surroundings." On the other hand, *The Varsity* was aware of the fatuousness that constantly lay in wait for those who sought to give prominence to all things Canadian, especially in the area of literature. With its concern for the native scene and its interest in Canadian writers went a warm receptivity to American literature, which, complained *The Varsity*, was completely ignored in the curriculum and slighted in the Library.

In retrospect, the decade of the '80's may seem like a period of bohemianism, Canadian style. Archibald MacMechan, a frequent contributor to *The Varsity* during this period, both as undergraduate and as graduate, reminisced thus from his professorial chair at Dalhousie about the "golden eighties":

We cultivated literature and published an anthology of our own immortal writings; we astonished the world with a new Protestantism. One oddity diverged from the regular prescriptions into heraldry and Russian. Our Shelley spent a winter in Paris, where he consorted with the people called Anarchists, and returned a missionary of the gospel of Henry George. We went to England as cattlemen, that we might stand in the Abbey in Poets' Corner and see with our own eyes those sacred places which had belonged to the geography of Fairyland. We read Sartor for the Blumine episode; we despised "gig-men"; our greatest oath was by Saint Thomas of Carlyle.

But, as even MacMechan's nostalgic recollections made clear, the bohemianism of the '80's was tempered by the earnestness and puritanism of an Ontario city. The young *littérateurs* of *The Varsity* were cautiously *avant garde*, discreetly aesthetic. They were respectful of the gods of genteel, cultivated society: Tennyson, Arnold, Longfellow, Lowell, and, with reservations, Rossetti and Swinburne. It was a good many years before *The Varsity* permitted itself to praise the arch individualist of poetry, Walt Whitman, and a response to the new "realistic" novel of

Howells and Henry James was slow to come. European literature went unnoticed, possibly because the French naturalistic novel had aroused in the Canadian mind disturbing associations of decadence and blasphemy.

What about the original literary contributions to *The Varsity*? There is much in *The Varsity Book* that can be read with a pleasure not entirely dependent on antiquarian interest, and no doubt a second anthology of equal merit could be compiled, especially if the choice were not rigidly confined to *belles-lettres*. Outside of the essays and the controversial articles, where the really solid achievement lies, the greatest emphasis was on poetry. The ventures into fiction were few and hesitant, the most substantial contribution of this kind being a short novelette by W. J. Healy. Healy was one of the most talented and most versatile of the *Varsity's* creative writers, being distinguished from his serious fellows by a gift for light raillery and wit. It was he, for instance, who in his satirical verses "A Ballad of Burdens" hit off the typical *malaise* of the undergraduate versifier:

> The burden of much Swinburne. Woe begone,
> With fleshly fever and amorous malady,
> Of wind-tossed hair, "sweet faced, wild eyed and wan"—
> He raveth in his sonnet melodiously;
> Of clinging, thrilling kisses raveth he,
> Of soft, sweet eyelids tremulous like fire;
> He sends his sonnet to the Varsity,—
> This is the end of every man's desire.

Whether or not the model was Swinburne, it is obvious that the undergraduate versifier immersed himself in a mood of pleasing melancholy before he began to write. The typical poem is a lament for a lost (and doubtless illusory) love, uttered against a background of sombre nature. One poet shook off these faded bardic garments, and that was William Wilfred Campbell, who was to *The Varsity* of the '80's what Archibald Lampman was, at the same time, to Trinity College's *Rouge et Noir*. Campbell was a prolific contributor to *The Varsity*—while he was an undergraduate at University College from 1881-82 and a student of Wycliffe from 1882-83, and later in the '80's when he was attending a theological school in Cambridge, Massachusetts, and serving as rector at a church in New Hampshire. These early poems of his, often diffuse and brassily rhetorical, show, nevertheless, a power over language, a technical competence, and a masculine vitality that raise them far above the languorous verses of his fellow contributors. It is doubtful whether the files of *The Varsity* can yield anything of more lasting worth than the short poem that Campbell contributed to the issue of October 21, 1882. Campbell's lines, coming after the prize poem for the year, a competent piece of rhetoric about the city of Quebec, were thrust into the final page amid a jumble of advertisements. It is the poem beginning,

> Along the line of smoky hills
> The crimson forest stands

with its perfect recapturing of the hectic beauty and the mood of mysterious expectancy of a Canadian autumn.

In the autumn of 1890, after a break of one year, *The Varsity* reappeared, now as a university and undergraduate publication, although it remained under the jurisdiction of the Literary and Scientific Society until 1901. Indeed *The Varsity* has always been a publication in which students from University College take a predominant interest. During the '90's it was University College students like Pelham Edgar, Stephen Leacock, and B. K. Sandwell who continued the literary tradition; and the list of University College editors is a long and distinguished one. Here are a few: James Tucker, editor during the controversy that led to the famous strike in 1895; H. C. Hindmarsh, editor in 1908-9 when *The Varsity* changed from a journal to a newspaper, and set as its original goal "an accurate chronicle of everyday occurrences"; Andrew Allan, whose stormy régime in 1931-32 closed with his dismissal and his eloquent appeal, in defence of freedom of speech, to the spirit of Milton; Hugh Kenner, who brought to the first post-war *Varsity* a distinctive literary polish. But, for University College, the first decade of *The Varsity* is most memorable. It was the period when the best things in *The Varsity* tradition were established: a good-humoured, but uncompromising spirit of criticism; a refusal to take accepted educational principles and practice for granted; an awareness of the University's multiple ties with the outside world. In addition, the early *Varsity* could boast a degree of literary consciousness and a level of literary achievement that the later *Varsity* never achieved, or, indeed, aspired to achieve. Finally, there emerges from these old pages of *The Varsity* a sense of devotion to the College that is deep and self-assured, that takes itself for granted and does not protest too much—a subtle but durable band that holds together those who live and work together in a common purpose. It is this spirit joined to a nostalgic love for the grey, turreted building hid among the trees that gives an authentic ring to the dedicatory lines in *The Varsity Book*:

> These songs fly forth to you, old friends,
> Who once have walked the echoing corridors,
> Or pressed swift feet upon the grassy lawns,
> Or drunk the spirit-haunted pages here;
>
> To wake again the memories of days,
> The vision of the happier days gone by,
> To wake again the murmur of the pines,
> To show the gray towers rising in the gloom.

Until 1908, when *The Varsity* became a newspaper published twice a week, it provided an adequate outlet for University College students who were interested in writing. There were a few attempts to supplement it, the most important being an annual called *Sesame*. *Sesame*, a publication of "The Women Graduates and Undergraduates of University College," was conceived of as a sort of belated vindication of co-education, and was, I regret to say, a consistently uninspired one. *Sesame* suffered from a disease that is fatal to undergraduate publications: an anxious concern for propriety and "good taste." The result was a dull, academic version of the Victorian annual. It lasted from 1897 to 1901; and, if valuable for nothing else, provides a handy distillation of the dullness and timidity that was even more a part of Canadian than of English Victorianism.

After 1908 it quickly became clear that *The Varsity* had lost its former appeal as a medium for the discussion of ideas and for serious writing. The loss was particularly heavy for University College. Victoria had *Acta Victoriana*, and Trinity, *The*

Trinity University Review, both with long traditions, but University College was left with nothing that it could clearly call its own. That gap was not to be filled for a good many years, but in the meantime a few undergraduates at University College turned their attention to the production of a University journal that would revive the characteristics of the early *Varsity*. The results of their efforts were two journals, both short-lived, but both blessed with ideas and with much vigorous writing—*Arbor* (1910-13), and *The Rebel* (1917-20).

These two journals had much in common; indeed, *The Rebel* may be looked upon as a continuation of *Arbor*. They were both University journals—*The Rebel* described itself as "the magazine of all faculties and all colleges"—but each was launched by a University College student and drew heavily on College talent. Murray Wrong, a son of Professor George Wrong, was the first editor of *Arbor*, and Elsinore Macpherson (now Mrs. Haultain) was responsible for starting *The Rebel*. Both—like the early *Varsity*—received contributions from the staff, particularly *The Rebel*, in which Professor Barker Fairley of University College, and Professor C. B. Sissons and Professor S. H. Hooke of Victoria were active. Both had somewhat similar editorial policies. In general they were opposed to the formalization and mechanization of University life: they tilted at student organizations that practised political intrigue and sponsored pretentious social gatherings; at lectures that stifled thought and initiative; above all, at examinations which choked off genuine intellectual adventure. They praised the spontaneous and the informal, and they acclaimed the small tutorial as the only genuine unit of higher education.

Of the two journals, *Arbor* speaks to the modern reader with a less persuasive voice. It came uncomfortably close to realizing an undergraduate's idea of what a university journal ought to be. Its contributions tended to be a trifle long, and to be formal in subject and treatment. But its list of contributors, viewed from the superior height of today, was a tribute to editorial energy and acumen. A number of eminent University College undergraduates made their literary *débuts* in its pages: N. A. McLarty wrote a compact and carefully reasoned article on "Canada's External Relations"; F. H. Underhill argued incisively in favour of "Commission Government in Cities"; and Ernest MacMillan explained what was involved in "Listening to Music."

The Rebel has, of course, a significance quite apart from University journalism, since it did not really come to an end with its final issue of March 1920, but expanded into one of the hardiest and most influential of the "Little" Canadian magazines, *The Canadian Forum*. Even as a University publication, it drew much of its vigour from non-student contributors: from Barker Fairley's reviews of books, more like clever, swiftly allusive talk than formal assessment; from C. B. Sissons' lively summaries and analyses of the political scene; from J. E. H. Macdonald's authoritative introductions to Canadian art. But *The Rebel*, in its general flavour, was an undergraduate journal of University College. In its pages, the spirit of the early *Varsity* was reborn, a spirit deepened by the tragedy of the First World War, but still permeated by the gaiety and rebelliousness of youth. Significantly, two of the old contributors to *The Varsity* of the '80's and '90's, now firmly established in the academic and literary world, pronounced their blessings upon *The Rebel*. "My paternal benison on you!" wrote Archibald MacMechan. "Pray, go on rebelling just as rebelliously as you know how to rebel." "It is a fine little paper," wrote Stephen Leacock. "I would to God, as St. Paul says, that they had one like it at McGill."

The Rebel, despite its motto—"Well, God be thanked for these rebels, they offend none but the virtuous"—could, at times, assume a serious evangelical note. It was concerned about the vaunted University College tolerance, which, it declared, was often only an euphemism for inertia, and it argued that enthusiasm should not be confused with priggishness; it welcomed a developing interest among students in religion; and as the time of its metamorphosis into the *Canadian Forum* approached, it became more and more exercised about the state of the world. But in its pages cheerfulness kept breaking in. Its stock-in-trade was the innocent fatuities of students, the diverting eccentricities of professors, and the never ending capacity of administrators for taking themselves seriously. (A basic theme is the scriptural authority attributed by registrars to the "calendars.") Here are two examples of the rebel relaxing and taking his ease. In a short piece called "Potted Student," there was an ingenious attempt to categorize types of students. The "Butterfly—general course," followed these general specifications:

French heels and Vanity case. Attends all class receptions, on class executives; goes to the rink for "bands"; favourite remark, "And he said." Skirts one inch too short, hats two inches too high, and worn over the right eye; with white, yellow, or pale grey spots. Movies. Two or more supplementals each year; light reading, "The Ladies' Home Journal" and interlinear cribs. Favourite professor, one who gives good notes, or one who likes the colour of her eyes. Leaves college with or without a degree.

Another type were the "thirsters," described in this way:

A small but excellently chosen assortment. No notes in lectures. No lectures except from selected professors; no religion; intelligent discussions at all hours of the day or night. Ideas and "the Truth"; light reading, Ibsen, brains, deep. Can be had with hats ancient and modern. One most attractive line very smart and guileless in appearance.

The second example of the *Rebel*'s genial humour is taken from a series of verse portraits of professors done in the Chaucerian manner. Among portraits of the senior and the venerable—Maurice Hutton, James Mavor, David Keys—appeared one of a young lecturer, who had already aroused the imagination and the affection of his students:

> A lecturer there was called Jeanneret
> Loved by his classes for his pleasant way.
> Busy he was, with many burdens pressed,
> Yet ever had a smile and ready jest;
> For French he taught and acted registrar
> And took his pleasure in a small Ford car.
> His fresshé hue showed him a goodly liver
> But he was reckless when he drove his flivver;
> And oldé strange bookés would he buy
> If Britnell's prices did not run too high;
> Corneille he got for forty cents or less.
> He weighed two hundred poundés, as I guess.

During the '20's there were two University publications in which University College students played important roles—*Goblin,* a humorous magazine which finally moved away from the campus into brief national popularity, and *The Privateer*, a new rebel in sophisticated dress, which had a brief existence at the end of the decade. But what concerns us most in the '20's was the emergence of a specific College literary journal. It had now become clear that independent journals directed towards the University community were hazardous ventures doomed to enjoy only a short, if exciting, life. Moreover, the students at University College were reawakening to a new sense of their identity as members of a peculiar and self-contained college community.

The appearance of a University College journal coincided, significantly, with the reorganization and revitalization of the Literary Society. The "Lit." had fallen on evil days: before the war it had deteriorated into a battleground for political parties, and during the war it had suffered from inevitable neglect. In the fall of 1920 a special committee, composed of members of the faculty and graduates, was established "to consider the revision of the Constitution in order to make the Society more representative and to engender a better college spirit." That committee brought in a report upon which the present Literary and Athletic Society is based. The report did not, however, include any recommendation about the fostering of literary (in the pure sense) activity, and it was to be some time yet before the "Lit." gave its official support to a literary journal. But, in the lively expectation of enlisting support from the refurbished society, a group of University College students founded a journal solemnly dedicated to "the development of University College spirit." In a mood of wistful self-depreciation, as if aware of its tenuous hold on life, it called itself *Patches*. Its early issues were slight juvenilia, even by the standards of college journalism; but in 1923 it acquired new editorial strength and triumphed over its uncertain beginnings. According to an undergraduate article on University College magazines (I have not been able to see copies of the later issues of *Patches*), "The literary quality of the magazine went up sharply. Its highschoolishness disappeared before a wave of sprightly and artistically-inclined maturity." In view of the fact that the editorial committee during these years included Louis MacKay and Robert Finch, it is more than likely that these comments are as accurate as they are enthusiastic. The direct descendant of *Patches* was *The University College Magazine*, its sober, plain-spoken title appropriate to a publication that was sponsored by the "Lit." *The University College Magazine* took up the role of the early *Patches* as a sort of spiritual cheer-leader for the College. Some concession was made to the idea of a literary publication, although the magazine depended largely, for both prose and poetry, on the contributions of one or two people, Nathaniel Benson in particular. By 1930 *The University College Magazine*, supported but not subsidized by the "Lit.," had reached the end of its tether. The farewell editorial was a bitter jeremiad against College apathy. This was the darkness before the dawn. The third attempt to found a College literary magazine was successful. *The Undergraduate* appeared in 1931, followed an uncertain course for three years, and then in 1934, declared the "official organ of the Women's Undergraduate Association and the Literary and Athletic Society of University College" and granted a subsidy, entered on its years of security. In 1946 it became *The Undergrad,* the apocopation, as Principal Wallace speculated, "a light concession to the spirit of the times"; it is now firmly entrenched—with an office, a continuing tradition, and a firm grasp on the interest of student and faculty.

The profile of *Undergraduate* and *Undergrad* was firmly drawn in the issue of 1935. Its immediate predecessor—the first *Undergraduate* to have the financial backing of the "Lit."—was a laudable but uncertain production: mainly formal year book celebrating and recording eighty years of the existence of the Literary and Athletic Society, partly literary magazine, and partly skittish comment on student activities of the year. But the editorial board for the year 1934-35—Gerald Levenston, Reginald Watters, and Douglas LePan were the leading spirits—knew exactly what it wanted, and, in large part, realized its aims. *The Undergraduate* was to contain only articles, poems, and essays that at least strove for excellence; it was not to concern itself with reporting College activities or with immortalizing student or member of staff in jest and anecdote; it was to aim, in format, illustration, and kind of type, to reflect visually the values for which it stood; in short, it was to be serious, experimental, a witness to high standards in literature and art. The list of contents for this issue established a basic pattern: a few short stories, a number of poems, a critical article on some figure or aspect of contemporary literature, articles on politics and economics, on one of the fine arts, and on philosophy or science, and reviews of books, the cinema, and the theatre. This was a stern regimen, and it is obvious that the editors for 1934-35 undertook their duties somewhat in the spirit of sadistic high priests moving among a mass of captive philistines. The leading editorial was unrelentingly scathing; almost every sentence erupted in a stinging epithet at the expense of the student body. The editors may have been reformers who possessed some of the unlovely qualities of the type, but they were clearly on the right side, and their aims, with some variations and occasional departures, have been followed by their successors. The most elaborate variation was *The Undergrad* of 1946-47, edited by Paul Arthur, which sought with notable success to make each of its three issues "as fine an example of typographical design as was possible in a College publication." The main departure came during the war years, when *The Undergraduate* for 1940-41, and again for 1941-42, became an elaborately illustrated year book with a literary bias, but not, as the editors for 1939-40 morosely predicted, a crude combination of *Life* and the *Harvard Lampoon*. Another departure was the ambitious, four-issue *Undergrad* for 1948-49 which, while retaining a literary emphasis, sought to lighten and diversify its tone.

The Undergrad has been inevitably the journal of a group. Any journal, no matter how vigorously it proclaims its representative nature, must be exactly that, for the majority of people (and students are no exception) are hesitant about embodying their precious convictions in words. And a journal expressly devoted to literature is, by its very nature, the work of a rather highly specialized group. *The Undergrad*, for instance, does not yield to the reader of today the same lively representation of student problems and aspiration that the early *Varsity* and *The Rebel* do. Even the articles on politics and economics do not bring back clearly the struggles of yesterday: their authors sternly proscribe the local and the immediate; their eyes are fixed on far horizons—on the Roosevelt programme of reform, the civil war in Spain, the Moscow purge trials, the downfall of France; and they approach their subjects in a grand and theoretical fashion. This is no doubt a healthy sign of the growth in the student body of an interest in international affairs; but yet one misses the lively comment on the campus scene that a less austere editorial policy would have encouraged.

But these are, after all, nostalgic regrets and not valid criticisms. *The Undergrad* was dedicated to one high purpose, and that demanded its concentrated attention. A more relevant criticism, often heard in the meetings of the "Lit." and repeated wherever two or three students forgathered, was that *The Undergrad* was in the hands of an "arty clique" whose watchwords were "obscurity," "morbidity," and "experimentalism." The contributor to *The Undergrad*, declared popular criticism, must conform to one type; he must be "serious, introspective and moody"; he must, in addition, have acquired some of the more obvious mannerisms of the fashionable writers of the day. Criticism such as this is valid, but not particularly damaging. Of course, the writers of *The Undergrad* read and tried to imitate their great contemporaries; of course they were serious and introspective, and consequently often unintelligible (to themselves as well as to their readers) and morbid. But it would be a poor college literary magazine where these qualities did not appear. The writers of short stories had obviously read Katherine Mansfield, William Faulkner, Morley Callaghan, Ernest Hemingway, and Sherwood Anderson; and the writers of poetry had obviously read Edith Sitwell, T. S. Eliot, W. H. Auden, Earle Birney, A. M. Klein, and many others: that they had read these writers enthusiastically and sympathetically, and had sought to transfer some of the power they found there to their own writing, is surely a proof of awareness and vitality. Although the editors of *The Undergrad* were especially receptive to *avant garde* writing, they did not, however, turn their backs on those who followed more conventional ways. What they feared most was sentiment and glib optimism; if he avoided these two pitfalls, even the most engrained traditionalist could hope to be included in the pages of *The Undergrad.*

The Undergrad is, then, not so much a mirror of student life as a proving ground for literary talent. In one of the "Forewords" that Principal Wallace wrote for *The Undergrad*—cogent, humane reflections that provided admirable models for the student contributors—he points out that "it is often maintained and with some show of truth, that Universities have proved but harsh step-mothers to the creative arts." We can console ourselves with the reflection that the student determined to write will eventually find an outlet for his work. But a journal like *The Undergrad* has made it possible for him to appear in print at an early stage in his growth, and to receive the encouragement and support that a college environment provides. The alumni body of *The Undergrad* and its predecessors has already become a potent force in Canadian letters: Louis MacKay, Robert Finch, Douglas LePan, Alan Jarvis, James Reaney, Colleen Thibaudeau, Henry Kreisel, Mavor Moore, Michael Hornyansky, are some of those who have established themselves with an audience far wider than the one they wrote for when they were undergraduates at University College.

It would be possible to construct an ingenious contrast between the students of University College who wrote for *The Varsity* in the '80's and '90's of the last century and those who have written for *The Undergrad*, and its twentieth-century predecessors; but the contrast would conceal an identity in temper and outlook: a love of the disinterested and flexible mind that glows most intensely in the great works of literature and philosophy and in man's endless struggle to understand the society in which he lives.

B. K. SANDWELL

Student '97

SOMEWHAT MORE than half a century ago I was an under-graduate student at University. The curious part of it is that owing to certain conditions which existed in the 1890's but have since largely disappeared, I did not then know that I was at the College. Or to put it a little more accurately, I was dimly aware that I was a member of University College, but intensely aware that I was a member of the University of Toronto, and a member studying in the Faculty of Arts. After I left the University I spent nearly forty years in other parts of the world than Toronto, and continued to think of myself as an Arts man of the University of Toronto. It was only when I returned to Toronto to live that I found that University College had developed a strong institutional character of its own, and that I should have to compartmentalize my loyalties. "Good old Siwash" was no longer good enough; one had to know which of the Siwashes one really owed allegiance to.

All this is not as surprising as it must sound to more recent crops of graduates. I had good reasons for being vague on the subject of the College. It must be remembered that some of the instruction in Arts was imparted by professors who belonged to University College and some by professors who belonged to the University of Toronto, but they all lectured in what was then generally called "the Main Building." I did not know, and I certainly did not care, when I was being addressed by a College don and when by a University one. But I was very strongly aware that I was not only a student in Arts, but a student taking the

Classics course, which I am afraid I regarded as the only kind of course worthy of the name of Education with a capital E. The vast present-day expansion of the sciences had only recently begun, and we of Arts, and especially of Classics, had some justification for regarding ourselves as the only true heirs of the ancient academic learning. We looked down upon the new scientific specialities which were beginning to swarm around us as mere trade schools. As partial excuse for this atrocious prejudice I may perhaps plead that the architectural design of the School of Practical Science, so closely resembling that of the worst high schools of the period, was calculated to produce in the mind of the observer an erroneous idea of the intellectual quality of the studies carried on within its walls. Architecture, as the Canadian banks realize, has a very direct influence upon prestige.

I was aware also, but not very vividly, that there were other colleges in the Faculty of Arts, and therefore entitled to respect, in the University. The trouble was that we never had anything to do with them except when their students came over and sat with us to write on the same examination papers. There was, for example, Victoria. I knew it existed. I knew that it housed the man who had done me out of the Prince of Wales Scholarship, and thus made me a disgrace to my old school of Upper Canada College, which was then not used to being done out of that scholarship except by other endowed schools; but I never met him until years later when we had both settled many hundreds of miles from Toronto in opposite directions. I heard also of a place called St. Michael's. Both these institutions had religious affiliations, and I was very proud of the fact that University College was a "godless" institution.

I was a Congregationalist, and the Congregationalists had not at that time been annexed by a larger communion; and the idea of exposing myself to the contagion of too close an association with Methodists or Roman Catholics never entered my head. Confident that nothing at University College would shake my Congregationalist foundations, and quite unaware of some of the problems which arise when religion and education are kept in too rigidly watertight compartments, I was inclined to deplore the fact that University College had recognized religion so far as to have morning prayers four or five times a week. (I attended them once during my academic career.)

So far as I can recollect, that attitude of patriotic loyalty towards the University and virtual ignoring of the College was favoured and tacitly fostered by the University authorities. Federation was still a very recent and incomplete event. Victoria had transferred its operations from Cobourg to Queen's Park only a year before that in which my class began its university studies. The total number of students in all the federated institutions was probably less than that of the present student body of the smallest of them; and the authorities seem to have felt that the distinctions between them, except those which arose from differences in the subject-matter dealt with, would gradually diminish and "college spirit" would give way to a wider loyalty to the more inclusive body. These were the days in which the dream of expanding loyalties was cherished in other realms than the academic; was not Imperial Federation being strongly preached in that very decade?

Of the feelings in this respect of the students of University College I think I can say with perfect confidence that we regarded ourselves as the one important, not to say essential, element of the University, the motherland of that intellectual empire. Our building, which had at one time been all that there was of the University, was still used to represent the whole institution whenever a pictorial representation was necessary. I have before me a programme of " 'Varsity Night" at the Grand Opera House on Hallowe'en in 1895. It has a beautiful woodcut of the "main building." All the office-holding members of the committee in charge were University College men. The chairman was R. F. McWilliams, for many years past Lieutenant-Governor of Manitoba, and of the ordinary members of the committee the six men representing Arts were all University College, with three S.P.S., four Meds, and apparently no others, although Dentistry and Pharmacy shared with these the privilege of having their yells printed on the front cover. It is significant that the College had no yell of its own, and was perfectly content in the conviction that it was the real owner of the common "Var-si-tee, Var-si-tee, V-A-R-S-I-T-Y" and that the other colleges were only allowed to share it by University College's generosity. Victoria does not appear in the programme at all, a circumstance which is perhaps attributable to the contemporary attitude of the Methodist Church towards the stage; or perhaps its students were too recently arrived from Cobourg to have acquired the habit of theatre-going. The show was *Trilby*, with Theodore Roberts as Svengali and Mabel Amber as Trilby, and in the subsequent parade most of the students carried canes about three inches in diameter, which had no function except that they made the police somewhat more cautious about trying to break up the demonstration.

In the programme of the 'Varsity Glee Club of the same year I find a coat of arms equally divided between the arms of the University on the left and those of the College on the right, the latter being simply a slight variant of the former, with the two books above and the crown in the middle. Here too the College had an immense predominance in both the office-holders and the singers. On the other hand the Literary and Scientific Society, or "The Lit.," while attached by its title to University College and using the College coat of arms, included in its membership the students of the School of Practical Science. (They were irregular in attendance except when the Brute Force Committee was called out on election nights.) This was no doubt owing to the fact that, while the connection between the College and S.P.S. had come to an end in 1889, and the School was now an entirely separate member of Federation, it had formerly been part of the College, and the Lit. would have had to sacrifice part of its name (and much of the fun of its elections) if it had ceased to have any "scientific" element.

However, the conviction that we of University College were actually the University of Toronto, or all of it that mattered in the "social and intellectual history" of our time, probably did not prevent us from having, as a body, a fairly distinctive social and intellectual character. In what ways it differed from the social and intellectual character of the other Colleges we should have known better if we had had more opportunity for relations with them. Unfortunately, outside of sport and the Y.M.C.A., our contacts were of the slightest. At the end of my college career I probably knew more about the Royal Military College at Kingston, to which several of my classmates from U.C.C. had proceeded, than about any of the sister institutions included in the University of Toronto.

Most of us, it must be remembered, had chosen University College in preference to any of the other institutions available in Toronto or Kingston, which had historic connections with religious bodies, and which we undoubtedly regarded as being more sectarian than by that time they actually were. There was therefore a strong selective factor at work to make us favourable to the concept of the secular university, and to the utmost freedom of speculation in all realms of thought. It was an era of immense and rapid progress in the number and size and repute of the state universities in the United States, and we naturally concluded that in this matter at least we were moving with the wave of the future.

Our disposition to question the proceedings of authority was not confined to the realms of abstract thought. Coming as I did from England, where the excellence of the work of the universities had not been greatly questioned for some generations, I was not a little surprised to find that many of my fellow students, whose childhood had been spent among the echoes of the violent controversies about education which filled the '80's, were entirely unwilling to accept the proposition that University College now represented all that was best in education in the best of all possible worlds. The period of controversy had been marked by the bitterest exchanges of criticism and denunciation between persons each of whom was convinced that his opponents had no real interests in education other than that of making as many converts as possible for their own special kind of religion. It would have been too much to expect that the adoption of a single piece of legislation such as the Federation Act, and the adhesion of Victoria to the enlarged institution, would remove all the suspicions and grievances which naturally

grew up in such a period; and the University strike of 1895 was the formal expression of an intensely critical attitude about the work of the University which developed among the older students in that and the preceding year.

The leadership of the strike came entirely from University College. Psychologically it represented the revolt of a new type of student against conditions which had worked well enough with the old type but were destined to become outmoded. The new students were no longer mainly products of a few endowed schools or grammar schools, nurtured in well-to-do homes. They were young men who had gone through the new high schools or collegiates which were just beginning to be capable of turning out first-class matriculation material. They hated privilege and nepotism as the worst of public crimes, and they thought that they detected a good deal of both in the University structure. The Victoria students would probably have been just as critical; but they were new in Federation, and they had to pay some regard to the interests of the Methodist body, whereas the University College students did not have to bother with anything except their own concepts of democracy, justice, and freedom. The particular incidents, appointments, and dismissals which provoked the strike at that moment were, I think, unimportant; what was important was a general attitude of mind in the student body, which would have been there just the same if it had never had occasion to express itself at all.

This new and more democratic student body—more democratic than that of any previous decade, for university education was now within the economic reach of any young man who was not under the necessity of earning a wage at seventeen and who had brains enough to acquire some kind of a scholarship or bursary —reacted rather differently from its predecessors to the cultural side of university instruction. There was, I think, a greater distance, a smaller degree of intimacy, between the student body and the really big men of the professoriate, in the Arts courses, than there has ever been before or since. Canada, a young country, had not had time to develop many native scholars of front rank, and the majority of the ablest instructors in the Arts

courses were Old Country men. This of course had been even
more the case in the preceding decades, but it had less serious
effects then, because the greater part of the student body were
from homes in which a good deal of the culture of the old land
was still preserved. (At Queen's at that time both the Old
Country instructors and the Canadian students were Scots, and
had thus a perfect bond of unity no matter what their cultural
differences.) The newer type of student at University College
was inclined to regard the culture of his English and Irish
professors as a matter of putting on airs; and the professors,
who were much overworked in any event, found it difficult to
get on easy terms with these rather stand-offish students. The
result, I think, was that the University actually contributed to,
or at least did nothing to counteract, that somewhat contemptu-
ous attitude towards culture as an impractical and effeminate
business in a young country, and that concentration on practical,
money-getting objectives which certainly characterized far too
much of the collective life of Canada in the first third of the
present century.

A professor, however brilliant, who comes into a country like
Canada after a large part of his academic career has been spent
in an entirely different milieu naturally does not rapidly acquaint
himself with the deeper characteristics of the place where he
has settled. He remains for some years an outsider, and hence
has difficulty in linking up his specialty with the problems and
interests of his new land. Roman history is no doubt Roman
history wherever it is studied, but the English in England do
manage to study it with a very sharp eye for the lessons that
can be drawn from it for the English problems of the moment.
The English professor in Canada requires some years before he
can approach history with a Canadian reference.

A generation later Canada was rapidly supplying itself with
plenty of Canadians of ample learning and culture, and they were
setting themselves to bridge this gulf between the teachers of
humane learning who could teach it only *in vacuo* and the
students who deeply desired it to be taught with a Canadian
reference. From then on, culture and humane learning ceased to

be a "foreign" fad in Canada and became something native and praiseworthy, since the possession of them obtained for Canada and Canadians prestige and even money from other countries. Culture from being an import has become a domestic product, and has turned from an oddity into a natural element of life. But around the turn of the century it still had not taken out its citizenship papers.

We undergraduates in University College were all very, very Canadian in those years of the '90's, but it was a rather limited kind of Canadianism. It did not take much account of the Province of Quebec, and it was strongly concentrated on the vast spaces of the West, so empty of people, so clamorous for settlement and development. Canada was in the short era of peace, prosperity, and confidence that came between the establishment of the transcontinental railway and of the federal authority from sea to sea, and the first tremor of the world's political and economic earthquakes which began with the South African War and are not yet over. The great influx of population into Canada had scarcely begun, but we could feel it coming. Gold was being discovered in the Klondike, Queen Victoria was celebrating her diamond jubilee, even the Americans were showing a kindly disposition and joining Canada in the setting up of things like Joint High Commissions. Halfway through the decade Ottawa acquired a new government of young men, in which the most energetic figure was a Westerner who was also a graduate of Victoria, and there were only sixteen years between Clifford Sifton's graduation and his entry into the Cabinet. Is it any wonder that our eyes turned very earnestly to the West?

There was a strong conviction that things needed to be done in a hurry—that vacant spaces needed to be filled up, institutions needed to be set working in places where a decade earlier the buffalo had roamed freely, the Canadian stamp needed to be impressed on a vast and virgin land. This was not a time for bothering much with pure culture; that would come later. Education, yes, of a practical character; political institutions, professional services, and intellectual leadership for the millions of muscular workers who were to pour into this land—these were necessary and urgent, but culture could wait. It was a perfectly sound attitude, for culture is something that has to grow, and the human soil must be there before it can begin growing; but it led inevitably to a rather low estimate of the social value of culture for the time being.

Actually I think we looked on culture as being entirely an individual matter, to be pursued individually by those whose tastes ran that way and ignored by those whose tastes didn't. There was very little opportunity for pursuit of it in groups. I spent two years of my university life in residence, but the Residence was too small and its population too mixed from different years and different courses for us to cohere into groups on the basis of cultural interests. There was, moreover, no common meeting-place except the dining-hall, so that the facilities for social life were not greatly different from those available to the students living in boarding houses; they consisted of the Gym, the Library, and the Y.M.C.A. There were also the meetings of the various departmental societies and clubs, but these were a little too organized and too much run by the kind of student who likes to get elected to offices. In my own time the English Literature Society, if that was its name, was a pleasant exception; Professor Alexander had breathed the breath of a genuine love for literature into it. Moreover the things that it discussed were things that you didn't have to be a specialist to enjoy, and people from all sorts of unrelated departments wandered in and took a hand in the proceedings. But these occasions were too infrequent to be a substitute for the common room "where men brush against each other and mould each other's lives" so much yearned for by Morley Callaghan's obsessed English professor of thirty years later in *The Varsity Story*.

That yearning—which by the way is the yearning of a character in a work of fiction and there is no evidence that Mr. Callaghan shares it—was certainly not shared by any of us in the student body of the '90's. We felt no jealousy of the Oxford men who were smoked at by tutors and slept with their heads in a tangle of ivy. We thought the University of London an institution much better suited to the modern world than Oxford, which we suspected of being designed for the express purpose of training men to be the last supporters of lost causes rather than the foremost searchers out of new truth. We admired and revered the Oxford men who taught us, but we did not wish to emulate them; they seemed remote from the world of practical affairs in which we expected soon to be immersed. Even those of us who dreamed of a literary career were inclined to fight shy of the old towers on the Isis, like Callaghan's other character, Tom Lane, who wanted to "take a shot at being a writer" and was "afraid of being seduced by the grandeurs and beauties of Oxford"—and who is as near to being Callaghan himself, or at least one of his Toronto predecessors, as any character in the book. After graduation these would-be writers of my time almost all followed Roberts and Carman to New York, where the vast increase in the supply of both paper and advertisers was multiplying the Sunday editions and the magazines. They did not follow Sir Gilbert Parker to England.

Looking back over that last decade of the nineteenth century I conclude that we, its undergraduates, were exactly the kind of undergraduates to produce the kind of Canadians who flourished during the first three decades of the twentieth century—until the Great Depression changed everything. Possibly we did produce them. Somebody must have, and we should at least have had a good deal of influence in the matter.

D A V I D   P .   G A U T H I E R

Student '54

IT IS perhaps just that the reader, who has been informed by Dr. Bissell that "the University College student has never been accused . . . of inarticulateness," should be given an example of undergraduate articulation. I have been asked to provide a representation and appreciation of the world of the U.C. student, emphasizing its distinctive characteristics. However, I am loath to speak for the undergraduate body; having cultivated an atypical outlook for some years, I must therefore disclaim any right to the pronoun "we," and write only of the impressions received in my first three years at the College.

University College students are perhaps more aware of their position in the entire University than are their campus contemporaries. Like the College of which they are part, they tend to merge into a larger whole. And not only do they merge, but they frequently assume a position at the centre of the University world. Thus an apparent lack of individuation itself becomes a distinguishing characteristic; U.C. students are marked by having a University-wide viewpoint.

The reasons for this are well worth consideration. The location of the College building is, of course, a significant factor; near the centre of the University, and dominating the front campus, it forces its occupants into a position of prominence, and prevents them from withdrawing into a world of their own, as can the students at the other Arts Colleges, situated at the periphery of civilization. Furthermore, the proximity of Hart House (combined with the lack of a student union) increases the participation of the men of the College in its all-University activities. A third geographical factor has been the location of the *Varsity* offices in the basement of the College, which inevitably has resulted not only in disproportionate U.C. representation on the newspaper staff, but also in disproportionate emphasis in the paper on the College's activities. The *Varsity* offices are now in the old observatory—still adjacent to the College.

The federal system, on which the University is based, also makes University College students aware of their wider affiliations. In the first place, their home building is constantly being invaded by students from other colleges and faculties, for lectures in subjects under the jurisdiction of the Faculty of Arts which are not given in departmental buildings are held in the College. And in the second place, their own lecture-room contacts both in and outside of the College are, unless they take only the humanities, with students of the entire faculty. Indeed, in the natural science courses in particular, the division of non-residence students into colleges is of no real significance.

Students are also brought into the wider Varsity world by the all-University organizations—political and religious clubs, athletic and dramatic organizations, and countless others—in which U.C. students play a particularly prominent part. Indeed, University College and the School of Law (which is to a considerable extent composed of the more vociferous U.C. grads) together tend to dominate certain areas of campus politics.

In conjunction with these forces drawing U.C. undergraduates into the mainstream of campus life, there are factors which tend to keep the student body of the College somewhat disunited. An Engineer, a Trinity-man, are well defined entities, but the term "U.C. man" (or, since the College is co-educational, "U.C. type") conjures up not even the vaguest image. Principal Jeanneret describes University College as "the keystone of the federal system"; I have attempted to show that the College students consider themselves the core of the University; but has the core itself a core? Are there any features characteristic of U.C. students, any distinctive aspects of College life? Is the student body in any sense an organic whole, or is it merely an aggregate?

I believe that it is possible to find certain characteristics, and even a basic principle, which do create a type of community, but before considering these I shall turn to the factors causing division.

The first is the cosmopolitanism of the College. Young men and women of every race, religion, and social class enrol in U.C. In a land composed of racial minorities, it is unquestionably beneficial for a college to draw its students from a sufficiently large number of groups that no one, no matter what its basis, can either remain exclusive, or assert dominance. Jew and Gentile, Ukrainian, Japanese, and British, all mix freely, without any form of discrimination. However, the College reflects the nation, not only in its composition, but also in that its various groups have not yet been dissolved into a unified whole.

The lack of a men's residence has certainly been a disunifying factor in the College, although, at long last, this need is being met. Whitney Hall and the Women's Union have brought the women into closer contact, but the men have had neither sleeping nor dining quarters of their own. That grand old U.C. institution, 73 St. George (now, alas, no more), was far too small, accommodating but forty students, to provide more than a nucleus of loyal U.C. men. "73" has always been a force in keeping the College together, but long ago it lost effective control over activities, as the overwhelming but inchoate horde of street-car students carried all before them.

In common with the members of the other arts colleges, U.C. students tend to be disunited as a result of their wide variety of academic pursuits. In a faculty such as Medicine, in which all students are enrolled in the same course, the undergraduates find far more in common than do Artsmen enrolled in courses ranging from Classics to Chemistry. Those students with similar academic interests are thereby naturally brought together; nevertheless there seems to be a radical division between one's relatively private academic life, and one's public campus life, a gap bridged only partially by those clubs formed to carry academic contacts into the extra-curricular world—organizations such as the Mathematics and Physics Society, the Philosophical

Society, and so forth. Thus any consideration of the students' world tends to leave out the essential aspect—studies.

As scholars, U.C. undergraduates are indistinguishable from their contemporaries in the other Arts Colleges. Artsmen in general may be said to have a purer interest in their academic activities than their professional colleagues, although it has long been suspected that certain "students" have no interest whatsoever in their work. These, it is to be hoped, passed away with the old pass course.

Having thus recalled the central aspect of University existence, I shall return to my digression on factors creating disunity. With these forces acting to pull the students apart, it is not surprising that University College has not created a world of its own to the extent that many of the other colleges and faculties appear to have. There are, however, certain exclusively U.C. organizations and activities which, if they do not produce a distinctive life, at least illustrate the somewhat negative yet frequently valuable characteristics of the College.

Undergraduate activity should naturally find its centre in the governing student body, but at U.C. no such single organization exists. The men's and women's societies have never amalgamated, so that student affairs are managed jointly by the venerable University College Literary and Athletic Society (established in 1854) and the less venerable but more sedate Women's Undergraduate Association. The "Lit.," the glorious upholder of College tradition, is, in common with numerous other bodies in all parts of the campus, undergoing a period of relative quiescence. The excitement of the years in which the veterans flooded the campus has passed, leaving a younger and somewhat apathetic student body in its wake, if I may be permitted a rephrasing of one of the campus platitudes. The Lit., indeed, may well be accused of becoming only an administrative organ, instead of maintaining its role as the voice of U.C. and the spearhead of College activities. None the less, the roarings of the aged lion still make *Varsity* headlines more often than do those of any other college or faculty organization.

The Lit. illustrates well many of the strengths and weaknesses of student life at University College, A few very energetic souls keep it alive; the rest are indifferent. It says much, though not always to great purpose; it prefers speech to action. However, it has always been accused of concerning itself with trivia, and it has answered its critics by pointing to the success of its officers in later life, thus giving proof that tilting with windmills is good practice for more serious struggles. Its counterpart, the W.U.A., has always lived more quietly. Women on the campus are seen, but seldom heard.

The most successful and characteristic College activities are cultural in nature. U.C. is marked by the presence of small groups of students vitally interested in particular matters, and larger groups of tolerant but generally uninterested people. Such a situation is, if not ideal, at least conducive to the development of cultural groups, which thrive on a few faithful stalwarts and an atmosphere of tolerance. At present, the most successful of these are *The Undergrad*, already discussed, which provides College students with an outlet in writing and painting; the Players' Guild, always one of the more thriving dramatic groups on the campus, and the training-ground of many fine actors and actresses; and the U.C. Parliament, the inheritor of the great debating tradition of the College, the most vigorous, if not always the most parliamentary, of the numerous debating organizations on the campus. Many of the more notable participants in the latter two organizations have gone on to win campus-wide glory in Hart House.

In addition to these three, there is Le Cercle Français, which owes its continuing strength largely to the devoted enthusiasm of the staff of the French Department; and two fairly young, struggling societies, the Music Club, and the Modern Letters Club. These various organizations have been weakened through lack of integration, a frequent failing in the activities of a college as diversified as U.C. However, attempts are now being made to remedy this by creating an all-embracing Arts Council to co-ordinate, strengthen, and extend College cultural interests. The other cultural problem of U.C.—the Follies—is being given careful consideration by the social directorate, which has concluded that the only solution is a completely changed show.

The College's remarkable athletic success in recent years is, I must admit, due to its happy amalgamation with P.H.E. (School of Physical and Health Education) for the purpose of computing points for the interfaculty championship. At U.C. itself, the great American over-emphasis on athletes and athletics is fortunately absent. A considerable number of students enjoy participating in sports; the remainder are quite oblivious to their teams' progress. The "rah—rah" brand of college spirit is not encouraged. Some outsiders have therefore seen fit to criticize U.C. undergraduates for lacking interest in their College, missing, of course, the fact that the students like the College because they do not feel forced to display superficial enthusiasm for it.

To analyse University College socially is rather difficult for one who since childhood has avoided most "social events" like the plague. The number of students, and their diversity of background and interest, prevent the College from forming in any way a social unity, although divisions do cut across racial, religious, and class lines in many cases. U.C. girls, unlike those at Victoria and Trinity, may join fraternities, and the Jewish boys' fraternities are quite strong, but fraternal organizations are neither politically nor socially a significant power on the campus, and seem, at least to this observer, to have little influence on the life of the College, although they do have great influence on the lives of particular students. Thus the social world of U.C. is, if less unified than some might desire, not dominated by outside organizations. The College tends to present the appearance of a large cosmopolitan aggregate composed of small, interconnected societies in themselves often cosmopolitan.

The opportunities for social intercourse among College students are, of course, restricted by the lack of co-educational recreational quarters, with the not too satisfactory exception of the Junior Common Room. (Indeed, in the University as a whole, lecture-rooms are co-educational, but dining and recreational facilities are segregated—a system of which I seem to be one of the few admirers.) At the College, there are several annual social functions—the Freshman Weekend and the Soph-Frosh Banquet, the Arts Ball and the Red and White Nights—which, if they do not arouse College-wide enthusiasm, do at least aid in bringing students (and staff) closer together.

It might seem from the cursory survey of College activities which I have here attempted that purely negative conclusions could be drawn regarding the U.C. student world. I believe that such a view overstates the case, and misses the values inherent in the nature of the College. I have tried to show that the student body is University-minded, cosmopolitan, and tolerant, composed of little currents of enthusiasm running through a sea of indifference. While some of these characteristics could be applied to other Varsity students—certainly the College has anything but a monopoly on indifference—in conjunction they are pre-eminently true of those attending University College. Such a situation makes it easier for the U.C. student to stay out of the University world entirely, for no forces are present to make him belong, to make him an active member of his society. On the other hand, the existence of groups of enthusiastic students in tolerant surroundings makes it easier for an undergraduate interested in some aspect of university life to associate with like-minded fellows, and to achieve, if not universal upheaval and mass acclaim, at least progress and prominence in his field. Also, the close conjunction of University and College provides a larger stage on which the chief actors can improve their talents before graduating into "reality."

The Reverend William Jenkins wrote of Unitarians: "We are not a fellowship of believers, but a fellowship of seekers." I believe that an analogous principle underlies University College, and unites its student body. This principle, usually only subconsciously recognized, is that each human being has a unique path to follow, that these paths are nevertheless inextricably intertwined, and that therefore the true community is that which enables its members to aid each other in seeking their individual yet related goals.

There need be, then, no set of beliefs, practices, or traits common to the members of the College for them to make a true community. Rather than seeking development on the basis of some uniting bond, they are seeking to develop towards a unity, and this unity does not exclude, but rather presupposes, diversity. It is true that the students have not fully succeeded in performing the actions dictated by their principle of association; they have learned not to interfere with their associates; they have yet to learn how best to aid one another. Furthermore, it is true that only those who have some path, some purpose, some basis for action, can help and be helped in such a community as University College, for no ready-made, stereotyped goal is supplied to its members. Those who have no goal of their own form the present sea of indifference. But these failings need not remain forever; a second century is beginning for the College.

I have presented a somewhat solemn view of what I consider to be the principle motivating student life in U.C. It must never be forgotten that undergraduates practise their ideas in the spirit of undergraduatism, interspersing moments of high seriousness with periods of inaction and of concern for the trivial and ephemeral. It must also never be forgotten that most human beings, university students included, reflect but rarely upon their principles of action. And so, having delivered these two caveats, I come to my final reflection: the student body of University College is the embodiment of diversity, and if diversity is a source of weakness, it is a greater source of strength.

F. C. A. JEANNERET

Idea

UNIVERSITY COLLEGE is the embodiment of an idea. It is a community of teachers and students dedicated to ideals of higher learning. As we celebrate its one hundredth birthday, it would seem fitting to ask whether it has kept faith with its founders, whether its aspirations are still the same, even if its achievements may sometimes have fallen short. If the examined life is the only life worth living, a little self-examination is surely a seemly anniversary exercise for a community.

Though University College is now officially a centenarian, in fact it is as old as the University, sharing with the latter a direct descent from King's College. Indeed, the separation into University and College in 1853 was even less real than apparent, the University assuming the functions of examining and conferring degrees while its College continued as its sole teaching body. Higher education was now the direct responsibility of the State, and the interests and objectives of University and College were identical. They still are.

Though the two have so much in common in addition to age and parentage, they are not identical twins. Through incorporation of new faculties, schools, and federated institutions, the University has assumed a middle-age spread, while its College, of necessity more heedful of its figure, has sought rather to preserve its spiritual elevation. Lateral expansion has even characterized the development of the non-collegiate section of the Faculty of Arts, through the increase in number of its departments, sometimes thus encouraging a reducing regimen on the part of University College; but this process is inherent in the constitution and does not imply any conflict of interests. College advantage independent of, or inimical to, the well-being of the University is unthinkable, as is the converse. We are one, jointly dedicated to educational ideals, and we have no other interests to serve.

While the century has witnessed some evolution in the University and its College, the latter has undergone no change in constitution for almost fifty years. It remains the Provincial Arts College of the Provincial University, integral to the state system of education. It has the same Board of Governors and administration as the rest of the University, with the exception of the federated Colleges, and a common purse directly dependent on the Provincial Government for supplies. The elder statesmen who framed the University Act of 1906, under which we are still operating, saw clearly the importance the College was destined to have in the University fabric. That University College was the keystone of the federal system in the eyes of those men of prophetic vision and that on its efficiency depended the efficiency of the University is evident in the following pertinent section of their findings:

The maintenance of the system of education provided by the State in University College and the Faculty of Arts in the University is, in our opinion, of the utmost importance. The division of the Arts curriculum into these two parts should not lessen the claim of University College for strong and sufficient financial support. From this standpoint it ought to be regarded as one effort, neither part being developed at the expense of the other, but both entitled to adequate aid from the endowment provided by the State. For this reason we consider that a common purse for the whole State system of education in the liberal arts and sciences is essential, and that the governing body of the University should also be the governing body of University College. In maintaining the college system the prosperity of University College must be regarded as a cardinal principle. Anything that would weaken University College would weaken the federal system, since this system is based upon the Arts teaching provided by the State, and the efficiency of this teaching is the efficiency of the University.

Our name was a birthright. But to some the first component was of prior significance, to others the second. Our Magna Charta of 1906 established for all time that the two are of equal importance. And only if we recognize our joint obligation do we deserve the right to continued possession of our century-old title. Could any other be as meaningful or inspiring to an institution seeking breadth of vision and freedom of the spirit? As a College we stand for all that we stand for as a University. Untrammelled by prepossession or tradition, to no code or creed confined, we belong to a community of scholars whose primary aim must always be the courageous and independent pursuit of truth.

Freedom from denominational control marked the birth of University College. But political independence came much more slowly. Before Confederation, government control was exercised in every conceivable fashion, and even long after education became the responsibility of the Province the Minister continued to make all appointments to the College teaching staff. This vicious practice was abruptly terminated by the University Act of 1906. Since that date all appointments and promotions have been made by the Board of Governors on the recommendation of the President of the University. At no time during this period has there been a single instance of political interference or influence in the administration of the College, either in the matter of appointment or in the matter of educational policy. The teacher has enjoyed complete freedom of expression in the classroom and in scholarly publication. His political and religious views are his own affair; and these same rights are, of course, fully enjoyed by the student. A real spirit of democratic freedom pervades every phase of College activity.

When liberalism is the concomitant of learning, the very breath of life is infused, and the College, still the stronghold of the humanities, keeps an open door for new truth and new intellectual adventure. We are the trustees of a great inheritance in literature and philosophy, the champions of the classic spirit, but we have learned from our study of history that tradition is not immutable, that truth and beauty have new facets, and that all that is good has not yet been discovered. A liberal education makes us love knowledge and cherish what is enduring; it makes us forward-looking too, eager to exercise what wisdom we may have learned in grappling with problems that present

themselves and zealous to achieve reforms that will make for the peace and greater happiness of mankind. Our ideal end-product was once aptly characterized by the late Professor J. F. McCurdy of the College Department of Oriental Languages when paying a memorial tribute to a former colleague, Dr. R. J. Murison: "I have never known a man who combined with such sustained and consistent devotion the seemingly incompatible qualities of a love for antiquity and an interest in the present; in reconciling so completely this antithesis, he was a typical, we may say, an ideal, University man."

The catholicity of outlook and of aim inherent in a true university must characterize its college. This has been encouraged from the outset by the frequent appointment of teachers trained in Britain, Europe, and the United States, and more recently by bringing outstanding scholars from abroad as visiting professors in all departments of the College. While the aim is to develop a truly Canadian institution, the student must learn early that there are no national boundaries to scholarship and that freedom of intellectual interchange is essential to the development of a healthy Canadian consciousness. Moreover, breadth of view is easily promoted among young men and women who choose to come to a college where they can continue their higher studies under the same non-denominational auspices they have enjoyed in the public and secondary schools of the Province or elsewhere. The first secular institution of higher learning in Canada still seeks to be a training-ground for adult life in the community by introducing no distinction in race, creed, or colour in teaching staff or student body.

There is one important distinction in status and outlook between the teachers and the students, however, and failure to perceive this often leads to confusion in both camps. The College professor teaches only in the field of the humanities, and he sometimes assumes that the student has no other interest. He may give instruction outside the College, in the School of Graduate Studies or in other faculties—still in the humanities. The student, on the other hand, though he registers in the College, an undergraduate institution only, may enrol in the humanities,

the social sciences, and the natural sciences both in the College
and throughout the Faculty of Arts of the University.

In this Coronation and Centennial Year—and what a truly
happy coincidence is so marked in 1953—a vainglorious note
might easily creep into our festive mood. Were we to affirm that
our College is the best of all possible worlds, we might even
expect a little indulgence, the more so as we have always liked to
think that constructive criticism was more salutary than praise.
But if for a brief season we resist the seductive charms of
cynicism and intransigence, sometimes only unsuspected indications of conscious superiority, we may discover that some causes
have actually been won. We have much for which to be grateful
to our constituency, the Province of Ontario, to the Board of
Governors, and to our friends and graduates. Their combined
generosity enables us now to offer annually in bursaries, scholarships, and prizes an amount not far short of $100,000 to
deserving and talented students, many of whom could not have
come to college at all but for this assistance. The academic
record of the present College generation is at least the equal of
that of their predecessors, especially in the upper brackets, and
their achievement is not surpassed elsewhere in the University.
Nineteen of the forty-one Rhodes Scholarships awarded to the
University of Toronto since their inception have come to University College, and the two recently established Woodrow
Wilson Fellowships were won by students of the College this
year. The yardstick used in these competitions to determine the
quality of our product is even more definitive than examinations;
all-round development of the student is more important than
academic achievement only. And now that our College is at
last to have a Men's Residence, comparable to that enjoyed
for so long by our women students, it would be difficult to
estimate the efficacy of this new and important factor in enabling
our men on graduation to live "more complete lives." Students
and teachers will have a still greater opportunity of becoming
partners in the lively chase after ideas. And this will be complementary to our new tutorial system, developing a greater spirit
of *camaraderie* and mutual respect by the increased give-and-

take of general discussion. The impact of mind upon mind will result in greater mental alertness, more precise thinking and expression, a more general intellectual discipline and moral toughening—a truly liberal education.

Because of our large registration, erroneous ideas have been entertained concerning the size of our classes. It is doubtful whether many institutions of higher learning anywhere conduct their instruction in smaller groups. This principle of breaking up into small units will also be introduced into our new Men's Residence, which will have six separate houses, each containing thirty single rooms for students, and each having a resident tutor.

While we are proud of our democratic and cosmopolitan community, and just as proud of the variety of our interests and objectives, cultural, political, and spiritual, we note with special satisfaction that of the fifty-nine organizations that applied for the use of rooms for extra-curricular activities during the last academic session, as many of them were for religious talks and discussions as for anything else. Since its beginning, the College has been animated by a deep sense of religious values, and it has given constant encouragement to the spiritual life of its students. It is not without significance either that University College is the Arts college of Wycliffe, an Anglican theological college, and of Knox, a theological college of the Presbyterians. Nor is it without interest that at this moment all three national heads of the principal Protestant churches in Canada, the Primate of the Anglican Church, the Moderator of the United Church, and the Moderator of the Presbyterian Church, have come from University College, as have numerous Anglican and Roman Catholic bishops, and parsons, priests, rabbis, ministers, and missionaries, representing all the principal religious communions in the Dominion. Surely it is fitting for a nonsectarian college, once called "godless," to draw attention modestly to this contribution to the religious life of the nation.

Our College stands on the threshold of its second century with cheerful confidence, still cherishing the ideals of its forbears, still hopefully and prayerfully seeking truth, wherever it may be found and wherever it may lead; hence in good spirits and dauntlessly intent upon finding a better way of life for a world that seems at the moment to be bent on self-destruction. If its students have learned something of the origins and history of the forces which have made modern civilization, if they have formed a first-hand acquaintance with some of the great master-pieces of literature, philosophy, the fine arts, and science, they have become better citizens of the world, and hence better Canadians, with adequate intellectual discipline to realize that "liberty exists in proportion to wholesome restraint," and that understanding, the antithesis of intolerance and fanaticism, is basic to the brotherhood of man.

The College has reason to be proud of the contributions its graduates have made to the well-being of this country. While it has steadfastly maintained standards, it has never sought to make its students fit into one mould, to make them little-Canadians or little-anything else. On the other hand, it has tried to develop Canadian self-respect and a willingness to accept greater responsibility. The toll taken in the lives of our students by two wars is testimony enough of their willingness to defend a democracy they believe in and to preserve intellectual liberty at a great price. An atmosphere of freedom does not beget uniformity in any sphere, and perhaps this is one reason why its graduates have played such a varied role in the life of the nation in church and state, the learned professions, commerce, industry, every phase indeed from the most humble, seemingly, to the most conspicuous.

It would be invidious to name names and impossible to make a valid selection for an honour-roll of more than 15,000 graduates, though two prime ministers of Canada and numerous provincial premiers, chief justices, and others of equal distinction might be mentioned. It would be equally difficult and gratuitous to attempt to define the ideal, or even the typical, product of the College. But perhaps no one will challenge or censure if we single out one category, the Chancellors of the University of Toronto, and leave it to all to judge whether these depart from the norm. Indulgence is asked if we call attention to the accident that only former students of University College are to be found among the graduates on whom this highest honour in the gift of the University has been conferred since the first election in 1876. Their names follow. The Honourable Edward Blake (1876-1900), Sir William Meredith (1900-1923), Sir William Mulock (1924-1944), The Honourable and Reverend H. J. Cody (1944-1947), His Excellency The Right Honourable Vincent Massey, C.H. (1947-1953) and Dean Emeritus Samuel Beatty.

University College belongs to the people of Ontario, but it is more sensitive to its national than to its provincial obligations. The College motto *parum claris lucem dare* suggests an even wider responsibility, to give light wherever light is needed. But if anything has been learned in the pursuit of truth, surely it is humility. Our aspirations have so far outstripped our achievements that it ill behoves us to try even to measure our contribution. But let us not lose heart; in our effort to light the way for one another, each of us may have learned to love what is good and beautiful and true. And as we enter upon our second century, let us still aspire to learn and to teach others to think clearly and independently, to judge surely, and to act wisely. Let us seek still to be a community without uniformity, to be a college with a university spirit—a University College.

University College 1953-1954

ADMINISTRATIVE STAFF

Principal   F. C. A. Jeanneret
Registrar   W. J. McAndrew
Dean of Residence   C. T. Bissell
Dean of Women   Miss M. B. Ferguson

TEACHING STAFF

Department of Classics

Professor Emeritus—G. Norwood
Professors—R. J. Getty (Head of Department), E. A. Dale, M. D. C. Tait
Associate Professors—G. Bagnani, W. P. Wallace
Assistant Professors—L. E. Woodbury, F. M. Heichelheim
Lecturers—D. F. S. Thomson, R. M. H. Shepherd, Mrs. F. M. H. Norwood
Special Lecturer—M. St. A. Woodside

Department of English

Professor Emeritus—M. W. Wallace
Professors—A. S. P. Woodhouse (Head of Department), R. S. Knox, N. J. Endicott, J. R. MacGillivray
Associate Professors—F. E. L. Priestley, H. S. Wilson, W. D. B. Grant, C. T. Bissell
Assistant Professor—C. W. Dunn
Lecturers—R. L. McDougall, E. Rhodes, D. Colville, J. S. Baxter, G. Cotter, R. S. Harris, L. Crompton
Instructors—W. K. Thomas, D. Cole
Part-time Instructor—H. V. Weekes

Department of French

Professors—F. C. A. Jeanneret (Head of Department), H. L. Humphreys, C. D. Rouillard, R. D. C. Finch
Associate Professors—W. J. McAndrew, E. A. Joliat
Assistant Professors—D. M. Hayne, C. R. Parsons
Lecturers—Miss I. G. Balthazard, Miss M. D. MacDonald, M. Sanouillet
Instructors—Miss J. Gillespie, J. Walker

Department of German

Professor Emeritus—G. H. Needler
Professors—B. Fairley (Head of Department), H. Boeschenstein
Assistant Professors—Miss M. J. Sinden, H. N. Milnes
Lecturer—R. A. Nicholls
Instructor—Miss L. Hofrichter

Department of Oriental Languages

Professor Emeritus—T. J. Meek
Professors—F. V. Winnett (Head of Department), W. S. McCullough
Assistant Professors—R. J. Williams, J. W. Wevers
Lecturer—J. V. Kinnear-Wilson

Department of Ethics

Professor—F. H. Anderson (Head of Department)
Associate Professors—W. J. McCurdy, M. Long
Assistant Professors—D. Savan, R. F. McRae, D. P. Dryer
Lecturers—J. C. S. Wernham, F. E. Sparshott, William Dray

LITERARY AND ATHLETIC SOCIETY EXECUTIVE

Honorary President   C. B. Guild
President   R. A. Bull

Literary Director—D. P. Gauthier   Social Director—R. A. Gould
Athletic Director—M. H. Siegel   Publicity Director—H. B. Geddes
S.A.C. Representative—E. Berger   4th Year President—J. R. McGill
Treasurer—J. M. Lewis   3rd Year President—M. L. Friedland
Secretary—J. J. F. Brown   2nd Year President—J. A. Millard

WOMEN'S UNDERGRADUATE ASSOCIATION
EXECUTIVE

Honorary President   Mrs. R. A. F. Sutherland
President   Miss S. A. Reid

Literary Director—Miss J. V. Seymour
Athletic Director—Miss J. V. Strickland
Social Director—Miss B. J. Menzies
Publicity Director—Miss J. K. Martin
Secretary—Miss S. J. Pitts
Treasurer—Miss C. A. M. May
S. A. C. Representative—Miss E. S. Scroggie
E. A. C. Representative—Miss C. J. Farquharson
4th Year President—Miss M. R. Gill
3rd Year President—Miss C. Schrager
2nd Year President—Miss E. M. M. Barnett
P.H.E. Representative—Miss G. Pegg

141

Executive Committee

Honorary President—Principal F. C. A. Jeanneret
Past Presidents—Mr. T. E. Jarvis, Dr. W. J. Deadman
President—Mr. E. A. Goodman
1st Vice-President—Mr. Eric Hardy
2nd Vice-President—Mr. C. B. Guild
3rd Vice-President—Mr. J. W. Gemmell
Treasurer—Mr. P. F. Turchin
Secretary—Mr. J. W. Westaway

Committee

Mr. D. J. Agnew	Mr. D. Gillies	Mr. L. M. McKenzie
Mr. W. T. Baillie	Mr. D. Gilmore	Mr. R. G. Meech
Justice F. H. Barlow	Mr. W. T. Graham	Mr. R. J. Phelan
Mr. F. R. Branscombe	Mr. M. Gross	Mr. J. H. Potts
Mr. M. Brody	Mr. W. R. Knowlton	Mr. D. Rose
Mr. C. L. Dubin	Mr. G. G. McCaffrey	Mr. R. B. Stapells

Faculty Representatives—Professor C. T. Bissell, Professor W. S. McCullough

UNIVERSITY COLLEGE ALUMNAE ASSOCIATION

Executive Committee

Honorary President—Mrs. F. C. A. Jeanneret
Past President—Mrs. W. R. Salter
President—Mrs. G. L. Carruthers
1st Vice-President—Mrs. G. B. McFarlane
2nd Vice-President—Mrs. A. R. Muirhead
Treasurer—Mrs. E. Stone
Assistant Treasurer—Mrs. D. R. Grant
Recording Secretary—Mrs. P. L. Baker
Corresponding Secretary—Mrs. G. Galbraith
Assistant Corresponding Secretary—Miss M. Fleming
Finance Convenor—Mrs. J. Hilley
Social Convenor—Mrs. W. L. Somerville
Scholarship Convenor—Mrs. A. Muirhead
Programme Convenor—Mrs. G. B. McFarlane
Membership Convenor—Mrs. H. Allan Fair

UNIVERSITY COLLEGE

ROLL OF HONOUR, 1914–1918

Hubert Gordon Allan, '09
Samuel Hall Allen, 1913–15
William Lind Argo, '11
Paul Lyndon Armstrong, '12
Thomas Andrew Arthurs, '08
Alan Featherston Aylesworth, '01
    (died after discharge)
Alexander Watson Baird, 1910–11
Fred Everest Banbury, 1912–14
Lloyd Ashley Banbury, 1912–14
Alfred Carbert Bastedo, '15
George Herbert Berry, '16
Norman Creighton Bilton, 1904–6
Montagu Herbert Bird, 1914–16
Gerald Edward Blake, '14
James Gordon Bole, '12
Felix Olivier Bolté, '16
George Gilbert Bricker, 1912–13
Albert Edward Bright, 1913–16
Russel Hubert Britton, 1901–2
Stanley Howson Brocklebank,
    1910–13
Richard Austin Brown, 1914–15
Walter Everard Alway Brown,
    1915–16
Leo Buchanan, '06
Jeffrey Harper Bull, '09
Sidney Smith Burnham, '12
George Walter Call, 1914–15
Arthur Henry Cavill, 1913–14
Philip Fred Chidley, 1910–13
Maurice Arundel Clarkson, '15
Ogden Dunlap Cochrane, '14
Stewart Cowan, 1907–8
Arthur Ramsay Creighton, 1910–11

Herbert William Mackarsie
    Cumming, 1914–16
Walter Howard Curry, 1910–11
Albert Edward Cuzner, '15
George Thorold Davidson, '08
Lawrence Lavell Davidson,
    1913–14, 1915–16
Harry Lyman Devlin, 1913–15
Arthur Clark Dissette, 1903–4
John Duncan Doherty, '15
Grant Douglas, 1909–13
Kenneth Brown Downie, 1914–16
Alexander Mitchell Dunbar, 1911–13
Arthur Jackson Duncan, '14
George Gordon Duncan, 1909–10
Guy Peirce Dunstan, '15
Jaffray Eaton, '07
Claude Elsden Elliott, '15
Joseph Elliott, '87
Douglas Quirk Ellis, 1914–16
Remy Bazil Elmsley, 1899–1901
Archibald Mackenzie Fergusson,
    1907–11
Victor Archibald Ferrier, 1911–14
Peter McLaren Forin, '91
Gordon Oliver Forsyth, '14
Roy Anderson Forsyth, 1913–14
Franklin James Foster, '14
Almin Minor Froom, 1911–14
George Gordon Galloway, '15
Francis Egmont Gane, '12
John Ure Garrow, '12
Gordon Smith Mellis Gauld, '15
William Miller Geggie, 1911–13
Donald Patzki Gibson, 1912–13

Stanley Hill Glendinning, 1913–15
Thomas Leon Goldie, '04
Stewart Marcon Goodeve, 1914–16
Ambrose Harold Goodman, 1914–16
Henry Andrew Gordon, 1916–17
Henry Russell Gordon, '12
John A. Gordon, 1911–14
Thomas Seton Gordon, '12
Oswald Wetherald Grant, '14
Angus Douglas Gray, 1914–15 (died after discharge)
William Henderson Gregory, '13
John Vincent Guilfoyle, '11
Edmond Alan Gunn, 1915–16
Murray Grant Gunn, 1911–16
David Elliott Haig, '15
Robert Gordon Hamilton, 1911–14
Harold Leander Hanna, 1915–16
Howard Kilbourne Harris, '09
William James Eugene Harris, 1906–11
Geoffrey Heighington, 1913–16
Maurice Russell Henderson, 1912–15
John Emerson Hill, '15
Henry Boyd Hodge, 1912–15
John Eastwood Hodgson, '09
Fred Holmes Hopkins, '05
Andrew Allison Horton, 1913–16
Ernest Dryden Hosken, '15
Hugh Lewis Hoyles, '03
Alfred William Hyder, 1913–15, 1916–17
Van Rensselaer Schuyler Van Tassel Irvine, 1915–16
Oscar Irwin, 1908–12
Robert Crawford Jamieson, 1910–11
Ralph Himsworth Jarvis, 1907–8
Sinclair Beatty Johnston, 1915–16
Kenneth William Junor, 1912–15
Ernest Reece Kappele, 1910–12
Hugh Reid Kay, '15
Thomas Ewart Kelly, '14
Henry Alexander Taylor Kennedy, 1914–15
Herbert Norman Klotz, 1904–5
John Henry Knox, 1914–15
Edward Joseph Kylie, '01
Henry Drummond Lang, 1915–16

James Miles Langstaff, 1900–1, 1906–7
Henry Lawrence, 1911–14
Alfred Edward Lawton, 1911–12
John Leonard, 1913–15
Melville Elliot Lobb, '13
Loudon Brian Melville Loudon, '15
John McCrae, '94
Lorne Hastings McCurdy, 1914–16
Hugh Edward McCutcheon, 1909–11
Archibald Walter Macdonald, 1906–9
George Allan McGiffin, '03
Angus McIntosh, 1910–11
Douglas Fraser Mackenzie, 1913–14
George Lawrence Bisset MacKenzie, '13
William Stewart McKeough, 1910–12
Arthur Edward McLaughlin, '92
Allan Pratt Maclean, 1913–15
Gordon Davis McLean, '11
Stuart MacDonald MacPherson, 1914–15
Henry Lawrence Major, 1914–15
William John Ogilvie Malloch, '91
Maurice Edward Malone, 1913–15
George Geoffrey May, '15
John Freele Meek, '16
Gerald James Wallace Megan, '06
Malcolm Smith Mercer, '85
John Redmond Walsingham Meredith, '99
James Gordon Moore, 1914–17
Donald Whitcombe Morrison, 1915–16
Francis Vivian Morton, 1913–15
Charles Alexander Moss, '94
Arthur Edward Muir, 1908–9
Harold Gladstone Murray, '15
Herbert Braid Northwood, 1904–5
Edgar William Patten, '16
Frederick Charles Peppiatt, 1908–9
Howard Vincent Pickering, '10
Henry Errol Beauchamp Platt, '13
James Edward Potvin, 1913–15
Harold Brant Preston, '14
Howard Primrose Primrose, 1914–15

John Alexander Proctor, 1914–16
John Henry Ratz, '92
John Stanley Réaume, 1912–13
Frank Bruce Robertson, 1909–10
James Ernest Robertson, '01
Charles Emmanuel Rochereau De La
    Sablière, 1912–13
Clifford Ellis Rogers, 1911–12
Evan Ryrie, 1911–13
Edwin Francis Sanders, '16
Stanley Walter Schreiter, 1911–13
Charles Bevers Scott, 1900–2
William George Stanley Scott, '12
Samuel Simpson Sharpe, '95
Alexander McGregor Simpson, '08
Ernest Alroy Simpson, 1911–15
Joseph Donaldson Simpson, '12
Harry Roy Smith, 1909–11
Richard Langford Smith, 1914–15
Geoffrey Allan Snow, 1912–15
Lorne Snyder, 1914–16
Kenneth Ian Somerville, 1914–15
James Campbell Sorley, 1912–15
Ivan Edward Soule, 1914–15
Gordon Hamilton Southam, '07
Lyall Arnold Stokes, 1915–16
Edmund Rochfort Street, 1894–95
Charles Elliott Sutcliffe, 1909–11

William Davidson Thomson, '10
Norman Ewart Towers, '08
John Archibald Trebilcock, 1910–11
Reginald David Turnbull, '13
William Francis Twohey, 1914–16
George Elmer Wain, 1913–16
Royland Allin Walter, 1913–15
Charles Harold Watson, '12
William Ogilvie Watson, 1896–97
Wilfred John Watts, '15
Gerald Edwin Wells, '16
Maurice Fisken Wilkes, '13
Harold Reid Wilkinson, 1910–13
William Hartley Willard, '15
Mark Webber Williams, 1912–15
Russell Williams, 1915–16
William Taylor Willison, 1907–8
Arthur Patrick Wilson, '16
Harold Mackenzie Wilson, 1908–9
Jardine Turner Wilson, 1914–16
William Robert Wilson, 1913–14
William Tully Wilson, 1914–15
Lowell Wallace Wood, '11
John Robinson Woods, '14
Benson Wright, 1913–15
William Jonathan Wright, '96
Harold Verschoyle Wrong, '13
Norman James Lang Yellowlees, '07

UNIVERSITY COLLEGE

ROLL OF HONOUR, 1939–1945

Robert Wendell Anderson, 1929–30
William Harold Kerr Anderson, '93
Jean Burgess Atkinson, '36
John DeLury Barber, '37
Robert John Barber, '42
John Malcolm Barnes, 1931–35
George David Beatty, 1939–41
Walter Stanley Beatty, 1938–41
Frederic Judson Bell, 1912–13
Gordon Eugene Bishop, 1940–41
Howard Bruce Boddy, 1929–32
William Michael Bowlen, '39
Harold Francis Burt-Gerrans,
    1937–40
James Alexander Crozier Carrick,
    1927–29
Robert Lloyd Chambers, 1942–43
Charles Alfred Channell, 1934–36
Herbert George Christie, 1941–43
Charles William Cooper, '37
Edward Morris Cowperthwaite,
    1930–31
Charles Maurice Crabtree, '42
David Alexander Cummings Crooks,
    1931–32
William Charles Dewar, '43
David Munn Dickie, 1937–38
Ian Macmillan Dowling, '28
Douglas Murray Elliott, '39
Keith Donnell Faris, '34
Chester Archibald Stewart Ferrier,
    1939–41
Robert Fleming, 1939–40
James Fraser, '33
Thomas Andrew Fraser, '36

Leney Herbert Gage, '35
Thomas Robinette Godfrey, 1931–34
John Fraser Gray, 1938–41
Meyer Greenstein, '40
Gordon Carruthers Haig, '35
James Frederick Mills Hall, 1939–41
Robert Wesley Harcourt, '34
Alfred James Henderson, '37
James Irwin Henderson, 1926–28
Ralph Ballantyne Henry, 1931–33
Theodore Herman, '34
William James Irwin, 1938–40
Marcus Harry Jackson, '05
Daniel Lewis Jacobs, 1930–31
Kenneth Geikie Jeanneret, '39
John Maurice Jewell, '40
Thomas Reid Jones, '35
Robert John Keast, 1941–43
Gordon Arthur Kidder, '37
William Lyon Mackenzie King,
    1930–31
Robert Edward Knowles, 1921–22,
    1929–30
Jack Nicholas Luscombe, 1942–44
John Kenneth Macalister, '37
Carson Alexander Vivian
    McCormack, 1908–10
Jared Vining McCutcheon, '35
Paul Clark McGillicuddy, '40
William Leslie Mackay, '36
Donald Alexander McMaster, '35
Wallace Spence Macpherson, '32
William Henry Magee, 1928–29
William Jamieson Martin, '39
Albert Harry Mildon, 1937–38

147

Herbert Elgin Mitchell, '35
James Russel Moore, 1936–39
Charles Richard Morley, 1937–39
John Forbes Morlock, '35
Carl Hamilton Morrow, 1932–33
Sydney John Moulder, '41
John Munro Murray, '40
Morris Campbell Murray, '40
Henry George Northway, 1930–31
Geoffrey Noyes, '41
Rupert Simpson Oakley, 1927–29
Peter Dean O'Brian, 1919–21
Thomas Alexander Oliphant, '45
Frank Gordon Paterson, '43
Gordon Paterson, 1936–37
Harald Smith Patton, '12
Edward Burdess Peart, '40
Hubert Frederic Pedlar, '42
Thomas Edward Powell, 1940–41
Ruggles Bernard Pritchard, '16
Robert Terrington Quilter, 1934–35
George Alfred Reid, 1927–28
Harry Reid, 1939–42
Gordon Albert Richardson, '41
Andrew Gordon Rintoul, '20
Reginald Francis Robb, '39
Edward Britton Rogers, '33

Arthur Rotenberg, 1939–41
Willard Hugh Rowland, 1935–36
Harold Elliott Rowlands, 1913–14
Oscar Hedley Rumpel, '36
Leonard Leigh Salter, 1929–30
George Percival Scholfield, '28
Thomas Paul Sheppard, '41
George Graham Sinclair, 1926–28
Robert Gordon Slater, '37
Ernest Hodgson Slingsby, '38
Anthony Larratt Smith, 1926–29
Malcolm Stewart Smith, '33
Lou Warren Somers, '40
Frederick Owen Stredder, 1919–20
Robert Philpot Swallow, '42
Harry Newell Tattersall, '39
John Terrace, '40
Edward Blake Thompson Jr.,
    1935–36
Ronald Duncan Weller, '34
John Duncan Drummond White,
    1934–35, 1938–41
Maldwyn Armon Williams, '38
William Ballantyne Wood, '39
Thomas John Wright, '31
Reginald Clare Yelland, '41
Isaac Zierler, '43

Lightning Source UK Ltd.
Milton Keynes UK
UKHW051059240722
406167UK00014B/655